DEDICATION

To Chris, Jordan, and Jensen, your love and support have given me more than you can imagine—inspiration to be better and the drive to never quit.

HONORING OUR WOUNDED WARRIORS
AND WARRIOR FAMILIES

Every day, 22 veterans—brave individuals who served our country—die by suicide. Heroes for Freedom Foundation honors veterans and their families by providing physical, emotional, and holistic support.

I am donating a portion of the proceeds from the sale of *Leading With Your Life Equation* to assist Heroes for Freedom in their essential mission. Thanks to them and the people who donate, our valiant veterans receive a warrior experience that would otherwise not happen...and I promise you, they are grateful. By purchasing this book, you're already changing lives. And I thank you.

For more information about the Foundation,
visit heroesforfreedom.org.

Published by Tomball Press
2101 Lakeway Blvd, Lakeway, TX 78734

Printed in the United States of America

philipjukufka.com

First Edition

ISBN: 9798429199221

CONTENTS

DEFINITION: WHAT MAKES A TRUE BADASS?

There are people I've known throughout my life who have made a lasting impression. Some of them have shared their stories in this book.

And then there are the elite, the people who step up, show up, and make things happen—every single day. These people are laser-focused on results. They are masters at helping people realize their potential. You know you can count on them to do what they promise. And to do it with 100 percent of their dedication to quality.

In my eyes, this is a "badass". It has nothing to do with physical strength or bravado, but attitude, work ethic, perseverance, resourcefulness, and follow-through at a high level. I've mentioned in this book some of the badass people in my life. Please know that it is a moniker I use with the highest respect.

May you be a badass someday with the help of *Leading With Your Life Equation*.

INSPIRATION

I can't tell you exactly when clarity hit me. There wasn't a singular moment when I recognized how the most important factors in my life added up to achieving my goals. But I'm sure it started when I spent summers on my grandmother's South Central Texas farm where she didn't accept anything less than one hundred percent effort. She taught me the importance of having a strong work ethic. My grandma had zero patience for anything she perceived as laziness. You did what you said you would, with no excuses and never quit.

I'm also positive that a horrific car crash in the summer before my senior year in high school factored into this same Life Equation—teaching me perseverance and the importance of defining what I wanted from and for my life.

There wasn't one "aha" moment where this Life Equation made itself known to me. But the drive to succeed and to overcome obstacles caused me, at some point, to look at those traits, actions, and skills that had proven time and time again to keep me on track and propel me forward.

Now, in the interest of full disclosure, I hadn't yet set my sights on leadership when I was a teenager. My inspiration came from the idea to be a part of something bigger. West Point was an honorable and differentiated path. Getting into this esteemed institution became a mission for my Dad and me after my best friend told me about it.

The leadership passion was ignited several days into ROTC Boot Camp at Fort Knox, Kentucky, my first step after high school, on my way to an awesome military education. Going through those exercises, I began to see the importance and opportunity of team leadership, to understand and experience, first hand, rallying fellow cadets around me in order to win together.

The passion grew while I was at West Point. Just look at the mission statement of the Academy: "to **educate, train, and inspire** the Corps of Cadets so that each graduate is a commissioned **leader of character committed to the values of Duty, Honor, Country and prepared for a career of professional excellence and service to the Nation** as an officer in the United States Army."

In retrospect, I wish I had taken the time to recognize the need for factors back in the days at the United States Military Academy at West Point—or even before.

I worked my way from the regular army to the U.S. Army Special Operations Forces as a helicopter pilot and team leader. Then I moved on from the military life that had been the backbone of my entire adult life to that point. The next step led me to grow a family and a career in residential real estate sales and marketing. I first served alongside teams of badass professionals and eventually built other such elite groups. And that's where I finally identified the factors that have been supporting me, like pillars, throughout my life. That's when I knew that a Life Equation, one that fits into your "Why", is a necessity for everyone—especially, any of you who are leading a team.

Building and leading motivated teams is my life...and this is my Life Equation, defined with action planning factors that guide me in my journey to change lives. To achieve it, I have focused on building and motivating teams.

FROM IDEA TO SHARED VISION

"What you want for your life will never happen if you don't make a plan and act on it.

You must execute or nothing will change."

The idea gnawed at me that I needed to do more than to formulate and live by a Life Equation. I needed to share my experience by writing a book. Like many would-be authors, I felt I had a message worth sharing—and hope you feel the same way when you finish reading this book. I can tell you that writing a book is no easy task. If you're an aspiring author, be advised that it's a long journey that requires commitment and soul-searching.

I was so excited by the idea of a book that I dove in, headstrong as I am prone to be.

That same spark, voice, inclination, or whatever you want to call it, was relentless. I felt I had something left undone and that was a powerful motivator for me. But its force caved under the weight of business growth that outpaced my wildest dreams. I put the book project on hold.

TIME WELL SPENT

In 2020, in the midst of the life-altering pandemic, I did what many people were doing: I re-examined my life. I think each of us sought ways to deal with the uncertainty in our lives. For me, I realized that the way my team and I navigated the many obstacles of the pandemic would be valuable beyond the reach of our conference room. I was living, learning, and leading a masterclass that illustrated every factor in my Life Equation. And the book idea came back to life.

I knew that this book shouldn't just be about my experiences. I needed to weave my past and my perspective into something that would be of value to someone else's future. In retrospect, I'm glad I postponed writing the book for a few years, because the purpose became clearer in that time. The message of "Leading With Your

Life Equation" became clearer and stronger during this time. The impact of my choices and the core values that drove them came into sharper focus. Or I was just paying more attention.

YOUR LIFE EQUATION, NOT MINE

I present the factors of my Life Equation, but you need to build your own Life Equation, not duplicate mine.

I realized that the book I was about to write needed to be an interaction between you and me. I had to find a way to do more than share experiences and pontificate about successes. Frankly, it's not what I've done that matters, but how YOU can use the knowledge. To help with that, I've included a section at the end of each chapter with a "Life Equation Lesson" to be learned.

I'm also bringing you into the conversation with questions after each Life Equation Lesson, designed to prompt your thinking and put the ideas into action. Use these tools to understand the process and to create your Life Equation. Come back to the chapter-end material. Revisit the material that you've read. Learning is a life-long activity, not a one-and-done exercise.

Always hold onto the reality that your life is a reflection of your execution—your choices and your actions. What you want for your life will never happen if you don't make an action plan and act on it. You must execute with precision and follow-through or nothing will change.

My goal with this book is not to hand off a Life Equation that works for me—which is cultivating my team leadership aspirations—but to inspire you to be purposeful with your choices. I will guide you through my formula while also giving you ideas for incorporating the factors to fit your goals, lifestyle, and passion. What works for me might not be right for you, but you'll be able to learn the process of customizing your Life Equation.

"There is no such thing as failure as long as you learn from an experience."

I'll share with you some experiences—both my own and those of people who have influenced me—that have directed and redirected pathways to success. Some things worked while others didn't, but they all contributed! There is no such thing as failure as long as you learn from an experience.

DON'T JUST SIT THERE

Leading With Your Life Equation isn't limited to a particular group. It's multi-generational. The common thread is the desire to master your life, to become the person you believe you can be. And to leave your mark on the world.

To get the most from this book, I encourage you to grab a note-book and pen, or however you like to take notes. Be ready to answer the questions posed in each chapter. Each one is intended to spark your thinking and to apply these concepts directly to your life. Don't wait and tell yourself, "I'll do it later." You might not, and then you won't gain the full value of what I'm sharing. Put this book down right now and get ready with your note-taking choice before you keep going.

> *"The common thread is the desire to master your life."*

Ready? Ok, let's move on.

The sudden changes in 2020 affirmed that action planning enables us to handle anything that comes our way. It might not be easy, but life will certainly be easier with an action plan than without one.

I challenge you to become indestructible, indispensable, and un-stoppable. Start now, by firmly grasping the intent to discover your "Why" and deliver results. Now is the right time, no matter who you are or where you are in your life.

+ CHAPTER 1

WHY DO YOU NEED AN EQUATION?

What do you want to achieve in your life? What do you want in your relationships, both personal and professional? Stop right now and come up with a list.

Now think about why it matters to you to achieve these goals.

How many times in your life have you stopped to really focus on what you want to attain? I don't mean random discussions with friends. When have you invested deep thought, delving into the "What", the "Why", and the "When"?

We all have dreams. It's the buoyancy that keeps us going, the hope that something better is out there and somehow within reach. We wish, we pray, and we keep dreaming.

If you don't create a means to that end, it will never happen. If you can't sit yourself down and commit to doing what's necessary to achieve your goals, then you will always be a dreamer.

You have one life. Do you want to rely on luck, fate, or destiny?

That's either foolish or lazy.

If you're still reading, then you have the desire to achieve more than you have to this point.

ONE LIFE = UNLIMITED OPPORTUNITIES

Greek philosopher Heraclitus said you cannot step in the same river twice. The water keeps flowing, taking with it anything moveable. Because it's always on the move, you cannot touch the exact same river twice.

Your life is the same. You will not repeat any single day. Each one presents a different situation, environment, climate, and people. Even when you go to the same job in the same office with the same people, no day is like the one before or the day after.

Think about the opportunity here. Every day, you start with chances to change your life. It could be as simple as trying a different restaurant. There, you happen to meet someone who offers a bit of advice that turns into something much bigger.

Maybe you decide that, on this particular day that you will stop waiting for a promotion. You decide to tell your boss that you are ready to take on more responsibility, that you want to advance. You take charge of your life, rather than letting things just happen.

Or you enroll in a course, sign up for skydiving lessons, go to dinner by yourself (yes, on purpose), or schedule volunteer time with a group you have emotionally supported but never stepped up to pitch in.

Stop thinking about that list of things you've filed under "Someday". Take action. Move forward. You have this one life. Make the most of each day because they add up to your lifetime.

WHY A LIFE EQUATION?

Your life experience results from choices you make every hour of every day. Even the choice to do nothing is a choice. Your decisions are important. You might not feel the impact right away. Going back to the bit of advice a stranger offered, it could take a while

> ## Some fires smolder, others ignite, but they all burn.

before you implement it and even longer before you see results. Some fires smolder, others ignite, but they all burn.

Think about someone important in your life and trace back to your first encounter. What decision prompted it? Did it seem like a big deal at the time?

Whatever influenced your decision, it was based on your core values—those beliefs and ethics that you hold dear, even if you haven't identified them. You make "the right choice" because of your integrity, honesty, accountability, or sense of fairness. You pick the tougher option because you believe in diligence over convenience. You pitch in to help others because service is a core value.

Your core values are embedded in who you are. Learn what they are. Use those values to map out your strategy for life. Be mindful of what empowers you, what sparks your joy and ignites your gratification.

Combine those core values into a Life Equation that guides your decision-making. With the power of your core values working together, you will achieve great things.

Or you can just let life happen. That's your choice.

LIFE EQUATION LESSON

A plan without specific actions and a timeline is a wish. If you want to make things happen in your life, you need awareness of what you want and why you want it. Your motivation must be strong enough to drive you. With a Life Equation, you formulate an action plan that gives you a measurable, purposeful path to follow.

FACTOR IN YOUR ANSWERS

1. *Have you achieved the goals you envisioned when you were starting your adult life? What are they? Which ones are still on your radar to accomplish?*

2. *What are your proudest achievements to this point in your life? Why do they matter to you?*

3. *Have you ever taken the time to create a life plan, with goals and milestones? If not, is that something you're willing to do?*

+ CHAPTER 2

MATH, LIFE, AND THE ONE QUESTION YOU MUST ANSWER

Before you turn the page to explore the concept of a Life Equation, I want you to ask yourself one question.

"Is my life adding up to what I want?"

It seems like a simple "Yes" or "No" question. But in order for you to answer it accurately, you have to dig deeply into your thoughts, plans, ideas, wishes, expectations, and goals. Before you can be sure whether your life is or is not adding up, you need to know what you want.

If you seek joy, define it. What would a joyful life look like for you?

If you want success, describe it.

You cannot embark on a destination without having an idea of where you want to go. When you see where you're heading, you can map out the best route. Think of a Life Equation as the measurement that checks your progress along the way.

LIFE AND MATH

Do you cringe at anything that sounds remotely like math? It's okay if you do. The process of creating a Life Equation doesn't require anything more than a very basic understanding of two simple math principles: addition and subtraction.

There will be no complex formulas, no fractions or decimals. A knowledge of algebra is totally unnecessary. If you think pi is something with crust and a filling, you're good. You do not need to know how to calculate the area of a triangle or determine how many apples your grandmother has left after making a pie.

Don't fear math. It's part of your life.

Every time you cook or bake, you use math to figure out how much to make, the amount of each ingredient, the right temperature and the time for cooking.

When you pay bills, you use math. The money left over after the bills are paid is:

Disposable Income = Income - Expenses

The math required to build your own Life Equation is just as simple as what you use for measurements and calculations every day of your life.

ADDITION

We've been using addition since we first figured out that two cookies are better than one. It's perhaps the simplest mathematical concept and certainly the most used.

For your Life Equation, you'll probably want to combine factors. Who are the people who add to your enrichment? What experiences bring more to your life? What character traits possess greater value to you than others?

What is the result, the "sum" of these contributions?

Addition combines things to create something greater. It could be greater in value or in volume, perhaps both. But whenever you add, you combine two or more factors.

Honesty + Communication = Trust

Curiosity + Motivation + Courage = Innovation

You + Me = Us

What will you seek to add together in your Life Equation?

SUBTRACTION

Subtraction is the opposite of addition. It is the action of removing something from the total.

Think about the people who take away from your life. Some individuals can suck the energy out of a room, deflate hopes, derail your plans, and cut down on your self-esteem, joy, success, and other positive elements. They need to be subtracted. More importantly, you need to subtract the characteristics that are the root of the problem. Traits like selfishness, unreliability, dishonesty, and laziness might be traits you want to subtract from your relationships. When you're aware of what doesn't add up, you're more likely to be mindful when you see it.

Remember, subtraction isn't always a bad thing.

Risk - Fear = Opportunity

Lesson Learned - Mistake = Experience

You need to understand the good and the bad in your life, what adds and what takes away. In the end, this knowledge will guide you closer to formulating your Life Equation.

Now, I could keep going here and talk about multiplication and division in life, but let's keep this to simple math.

WHAT THE "*f*" IS THIS?

Your Life Equation could be a combination of various factors. Mine is:

$$m\ (T) = f\ (P^2 + t + s + a)$$

Translated, it says:

*A motivated team [m(T)] is the function of passionate people (P²),
who are well trained (t), organized around strategy (s),
and committed to full accountability (a).*

My Life Equation is mostly addition. The P^2 is multiplication, meaning P x P.

But what's that "f"? It's not just a pretty way to write the letter "f". It means "function". When you have a bunch of factors with equal weight, you can gather them between a set of parentheses and put that function symbol in front of it. This combination means that everything between those parentheses is treated as one thing. Think of it like a bouquet of flowers. You have a bunch of stems with different buds, blooms, or leaves. Individually, they are their own flower. Together, they are a bouquet, something that presents a whole different feeling and experience.

Your Life Equation math lesson is now over. Let's get into exploring how to take control of your life and make sure it adds up to what you want!

LIFE EQUATION LESSON

Math is part of life. You use it everyday, whether you're aware of it or not. A Life Equation is a matter of identifying what you want to achieve and then pulling together the factors that will guide you there. It's a measuring stick and a roadmap that keeps you on track, as long as you remain committed to following it.

FACTOR IN YOUR ANSWERS

1. *Using addition, what factors add up to "Happiness" for you?*

2. *Using subtraction, what is the result when you subtract "Procrastination" from "Planning"?*

+ CHAPTER 3

THE TREE THAT CHANGED MY LIFE

Where are the defining moments in your life that signal a crossroad, that point where a single decision alters your path? Do you even know at the time that it's a life-changer?

Life can move along so smoothly that you don't realize how easy you have it. Then, with one choice, one reaction, and in one solitary instant, upheaval occurs. It's like the magician who yanks a tablecloth from beneath the china placed on top of it. The settings magically stay in place. But then another person tries, and all of those fragile items tumble and shatter.

For me, it was a tree that yanked everything from underneath me. A tree changed my life.

At the age of 16, I did something totally normal that turned out to be a defining moment. It happened in the summer of 1987, in my hometown of Tomball, Texas, just before I entered my senior year in high school, I was hanging out for a bit after finishing football practice. My teammate, Matt, offered me a ride home after the exhausting practice. I climbed in the back seat of my teammate's car, along with two other friends.

On the drive home, Matt became impatient with the slow-moving car in front of us. He moved to the opposite lane on the two-lane road. Instantly, he saw an oncoming car. The passenger next to him saw it, too, and reacted by grabbing the steering wheel. Matt lost control. The car swerved and smashed into a tree. It struck with such force that the vehicle actually launched upward and hung in the tree, about five feet off the ground. The force of the impact propelled me under the driver's seat. A large branch came loose and smashed the roof of the car, right above where I was stuffed.

Surprisingly, the three other teens in the car emerged with only minor injuries. The first responders, however, had to use the jaws of life to extract me from the car. Unconscious, I was rushed to the hospital.

My body was beaten, severely bruised, with deep lacerations as a result of the trauma. I suffered a brain concussion, dislocated my shoulder, and my arm required 26 stitches. I was a mess.

After the crash, I had remained unconscious for what the doctors called "an undetermined amount of time." It could have been 30 minutes, maybe longer. No one clocked it. When I awoke in the ICU, a woman was bawling her eyes out while holding but holding firmly to my hand as the doctor stitched up a gash on my arm.

I didn't know who this crying lady was. She told me, but it didn't register right then. In fact, it took a little time before my brain finally emerged from that cloud and recognized my mom. After that, she had to prompt me with the names of my visitors because I didn't remember them either.

The prognosis at the time was recovery, but with lots of questions. When the doctors questioned my ability to play football, I decided then and there to prove them wrong. I had to rebuild my battered body, which took long hours of grueling physical therapy. I was in great physical shape when I got in Matt's car that day. I saw no reason why I couldn't get myself back to that peak condition. It took a lot of work, but I stayed focused on where I wanted to be,

> **West Point wasn't a wish or a dream. It was a plan.**

not looking back at what had happened.

I was lucky, very lucky, in the eyes of the people around me. I survived a horrific crash with no lingering effects. Well, almost none.

A TIGHTLY WOVEN PLAN UNRAVELS

That summer, I was pursuing a dream beyond high school football. And if you know anything about Texas, you know that high school football isn't merely a game. It's the shining beacon of Friday night lights, where a local kid becomes a hero, a name that is forever etched in the annals of the town's proud heritage. I loved football, and it was part of my forthcoming plans, but just a part.

I had already applied to the United States Military Academy at West Point. Unlike college admissions, West Point requires an accepted application and a nomination by a member of Congress. I intended to play football there and to then serve my country as an officer in the U.S. Army. It wasn't a wish or a dream. In my mind, it was a plan.

But then there was that tree. More specifically, there was the fact that no one knew how long I was unconscious. Here's a tidbit you probably didn't know about West Point admissions—and one that I learned all too soon. The Department of Defense (DoD) Medical Review Board must approve all admissions to West Point. When my medical record was submitted and included the notation that I had been knocked "unconscious for an undetermined amount of time", I received a *mandatory medical disqualification.* I was advised I had to wait two years from the incident before I could re-apply.

Two years is a lifetime to an active, driven teenager. I was derailed. I read and reread the letter that dashed my dreams, desperate to find hope.

I had planned to complete my senior year in high school with the crystal clear view of my future at West Point . But that was no longer an option. Sure, I could attend a college or university, but that didn't appeal to me in the least. That alternative was an "out" that I wasn't willing to explore.

I searched for options that would somehow bring me back around to my goal of attending West Point. I contacted their admissions counselor and said, "What would you do if you were me?"

He sensed both my determination and heartache. He told me I could attend a military junior college during my two-year wait. Ok, that's a positive step. I drove with my parents to Marion Military Institute, a small junior college with only a few hundred cadets enrolled, just outside of Selma, Alabama. I was accepted and felt exuberant—and relieved—that I was making headway. I hadn't given up on my goal of West Point so I was still moving forward.

PAYING MY WAY

While I was a cadet at Marion, I had the opportunity to undertake training for the Reserved Officers' Training Corps—ROTC. I showed up at boot camp at Fort Knox, Kentucky, ready to work. I reported for my medical exam and traditional buzz cut. Then, while I stood in line at attention, the drill sergeant pulled me from the ranks. He looked at me curiously and commanded, "Why are you here? You have a medical disqualification."

He explained that I would not be eligible for a ROTC scholarship, which meant I would not receive the scholarship or military pay during the training. I also had to sign a waiver that the military would carry no risk for me. As I was not yet 18 at the time, I also had to have my parents' signatures on the waiver.

Heartbroken once again, I called home and explained the latest obstacle.

> *"I wanted to be back home and let my mother smother me with sympathy.*
>
> *But I also knew Dad was right."*

My mother urged me to pack up and come home. She then handed the receiver to my father. I didn't hear anything, but I knew he was there. When he spoke, Dad asked me in a calm tone, "Let me ask you a question, son, why are you there in the first place?"

> **I could have made other choices. In my heart, those would be compromises.**

I'll be honest. I wanted to run away. I wanted to be back home and let my mother smother me with sympathy. I was extremely pissed off at what I was hearing from my father, but I also knew Dad was right. My father is a quiet man, but he has always had an uncanny ability to assess a situation and make the right choice, no matter how tough that decision was.

Dad told me it was wrong to quit. He advised me to stick it out. If, at the end of the school year, I still wanted to come home, he would support that decision. And then he left it up to me.

I completed ROTC, with honors, and returned to Marion Military Institute. My Professor of Military Science (PMS) there told me that I could file for a waiver by the DoD Medical Review Board. If granted, the waiver would grant the ROTC scholarship, even though I had already completed the training. Another good omen!

In the fall of my second and final year there, I received another letter from the Department of Defense. My heart pounded when I saw the return address and I paused, fearing to see what was inside.

The letter advised me that the DoD approved my waiver. I was granted the ROTC scholarship and they backdated it to cover my entire ROTC training expense. Soon after, I also received the nomination from both Senator Lloyd Bentsen and Congressman Joe Barton for appointment to the U.S. Military Academy at West Point.

ANOTHER LEAP

I was accepted but had one more hurdle. West Point is a four-year institution. My PMS at Marion Military Institute told me that, although I would complete two years at the junior military academy, I would enter West Point as a freshman. Starting over this way also meant that I would have to resign my commission as 2nd Lieutenant that I had earned at Marion. With the commission, I could begin earning an income in the Reserve while attending a four-year university.

This decision prompted another call to my parents. Once again, Dad took the tough approach. "Son, didn't you do all this to get into the military academy?"

He was right. I couldn't back down. In truth, it wasn't a hard decision.

I told my PMS, "With all due respect, I'm going to elect to go to the U.S. Military Academy. I will resign my officer's commission."

Here's the thing. I could have made other choices. I **could have** enrolled in a public or private college right after high school. I **could have** gone into the U.S. Army Reserve and major university after graduating from Marion. But, in my heart, those options were compromises.

I matured. The two years invested in Marion Military Institute paid a dividend. The experience shaped me for the four years to follow. I didn't take the major leap from high school grad to West Point plebe, but instead had the opportunity to gradually ready myself to face the challenge there.

West Point is strict and demanding—both physically and mentally. It must be. They're training leaders who will be responsible for many lives. There's no room for doubt about a single cadet. Without the experience that boosted both my physical and mental toughness, I likely would have been among the many cadets who "step left", failing at West Point.

Colliding with that tree in 1987 was an accident. But it started me on a path filled with purpose.

LIFE EQUATION LESSON

You never know what lies ahead. You can plan carefully and consider all contingencies, but challenges and obstacles will come into your path. Don't waste time wallowing on what happened. Channel your energy into seeking and implementing a solution. Learn from whatever pushed you off-course. Correct. And push forward.

FACTOR IN YOUR ANSWERS

1. *Do you believe in luck, both good and bad? What are some of the experiences that you think resulted from luck?*

2. *If you could go back and change one decision in your life, what would that be? What outcome would you hope from that altered decision? How would that change where you are now?*

+ CHAPTER 4

TEAMS AND TEAMWORK: WHY YOU NEED THEM AND WHAT MAKES THEM TICK

$$\mathbf{m\ (T)} = f\ (P^2 + t + s + a)$$

Poet John Donne wrote, "No man is an island." A few words but powerful—and true.

You are a member of many teams, whether you know it or not. We ALL are. A team could be you and your family, you and your significant other, you and your close friends, and you and your co-workers. A team is simply a group of people who share a common thread. The members support one another. Together, they make one another better and mutually accountable.

Well, they should.

You belong to teams, with different expectations in each one. How many do you lead? You don't always have to be the one in charge. Leadership comes in many styles. You could be strong and commanding or someone who nudges and gently guides others. Or something else. But the one common factor is that in order to lead, you must have followers, and that means you're part of a team.

KNOW YOUR ROLE

How do you use your various teams? What part do you play? What do you give and what do you get?

YOUR PLAYBOOK

Look at the many teams you "play" on. Write them down so you can see. Then ask yourself:

1. "What does this team do for its members?"

2. "What do I contribute to this team?"

3. "What do they expect of me?"

You probably know many dysfunctional teams. The people in that group aren't in sync with one another. Maybe there's one (or more) toxic members who disrupt the flow. A team is only as good as its weakest member.

WHO DESERVES A SPOT ON YOUR TEAM?

Have you taken the time to define the necessary ingredients of YOUR teams? Who will contribute to the goals you've set forth for this group?

> *"A team is only as good as its weakest member."*

First and foremost, teammates need to understand and embrace your "why". They must share your purpose to keep the team's actions aligned. My own motivation is changing people's lives. To

" **A team is a group of people who share a common thread.**

Together, they make one another better. "

do it, I need teams of people who are passionate and who share this desire.

It's one thing to assemble a team. Bringing them together is not the same as making sure they have the right fundamental ingredients. It's like a ship without a rudder. How is it going to navigate the waters? The ship might not go anywhere or it might even sink.

Former Major League all-star pitcher Roger Clemens was a dominant force during his 22 seasons in the majors. During his career, the "Rocket" earned 354 wins, struck out a staggering 4,672 batters, and achieved an ERA (Earned Run Average) of 3.12—a stat that any pitcher would love next to their name. He was an All-Star 11 times, won seven Cy Young Awards (Best PItcher), and played on two World Series championship teams.

I first connected with Roger after he and his wife, Debbie, bought a home at one of our Legacy International resort communities. He asked about the company and was interested to learn about my Texas roots and military background. We spoke on the phone a few times and then met at a foundation fundraiser he was hosting.

We partnered at two Warrior Foundation golf tournaments. During our time together, I've learned a lot about Roger's road to success. He knows what it takes and what it means to win. We've talked about the importance of a Life Equation. He believes that success is the combination of factors.

> *"Along with God-given talent, you have to check off other boxes: your willpower, your drive, your determination, your staying power."*
>
> —Roger Clemens

We recently talked about Roger's rise in the big leagues. He had talent but needed to do a lot more to put that into the equation for success. His approach to life is what makes him a badass, in my opinion.

"When someone says he or she has God-given talent, to me, that doesn't mean you just showed up and everything works out for you. Along with that God-given talent, you have to check off other boxes: your willpower, your drive, your determination, your durability—staying power—and being a team player. All of these things make those around you better and help them elevate their game, taking them to a level where they never knew they could go."

TEAM-BUILDING: MORE THAN AN EXERCISE

Now that you have a good view of your teams and teammates, how do you build teamwork? If you can't execute successfully as a team, you've got some work to do.

There are plenty of ways to build teamwork. I know the popular idea is getting people together to go through a series of games and exercises. It's a great activity. Just not a lasting one.

"Teamwork, like trust, builds over time."

Those kinds of team-building days and retreats are like New Year's resolutions. You're all worked up in the moment and for a short time later. Then you fall back into old habits. Maybe that guy with whom you made amends at the team-building event starts getting on your nerves again. You avoid him or confront him, depending on your personality. Either way, you've probably forgotten the lessons learned in that long-ago team-building exercise.

The proof of effective teamwork comes a long time after the "trust catch" and role-playing games are over.

Teamwork, like trust, builds over time. The most successful teams I've ever seen practice over and over. In the Special Ops Aviation Regiment (SOAR), we trained on every aspect of a mission, down to the last detail. We repeated every step until it was automatic and within plus-or-minus 30 seconds of the target completion time. A civilian might see this as excessive. But we knew that the slightest misstep or going just 10 seconds beyond the expected time could mean life or death. Gives a new meaning to "overkill".

MY PLAYING FIELD

I love football. I'm a Texan and loving this sport is part of our DNA. Friday Night Lights during football season are as sacred to a Texan as barbecue.

The sport also demonstrates the power of teamwork. If you're not a fan of football, please bear with me for a bit. You'll understand.

The quarterback is the team's leader. He chooses and calls the plays, communicating them to his teammates, who have practiced each play countless times.

For a passing play, the quarterback steps back and launches the ball to a spot down field. He knows his target exactly. He's not throwing to the receiver but to the place where that player is expected to be. In other words, the QB focuses on the execution, not the individual.

Meanwhile, the intended receiver moves through the throng of blockers to get to the appointed spot. He doesn't need to watch the QB. He knows from drill after drill where he needs to be, and that's his only target. With perfect execution—which includes dodging tackles—the receiver reaches up and catches the ball. It's absolute synchronicity.

PRACTICE × PRACTICE = CONFIDENCE

The exacting execution that occurs on the playing field requires practice, and lots of it. It also relies on confidence that teammates have for one another. The quarterback has confidence that his linemen are going to protect him from the massive bodies rushing to tackle him. It's their job to keep the threat at bay while the quarterback executes his own actions. He also relies on the receiver's ability to shake off the defense and get where he needs to be in order to catch the pass.

I won't bore the non-football lovers with some of the best all-time duos of quarterback and receiver. The rest of you already have opinions on those pairings. But when the magic happens between teammates, it's a beautiful thing.

Every member of the team must have this level of confidence in the other players. Doubt leads to second-guessing. Doubt causes an unexpected shift that throws off the rest of the group.

A quarterback who isn't confident that a receiver can catch and hold onto the ball will choose another receiver. If that confidence can't be built, one of the two will be benched—probably the receiver.

> *"Doubt leads to second-guessing.*
>
> *Doubt causes an unexpected shift that throws off the rest of the team."*

In business, your playbook is similar. You and your team complete a series of plays designed to achieve a score. You practice over and over to execute the play flawlessly. You work through the "What if's" and put contingency plans in place.

No matter what happens on your playing field, it is the direct result of teamwork. Catch or fumble, score or miss, break through tackles, and dash for the end zone or go down—it's a team effort. With a team, no one person is responsible for winning or losing. Either way, you're all in it together.

Confidence doesn't happen instantaneously when players step onto the field. It's cultivated, strengthened with each successful execution of a play.

> *"With a team, no one person is responsible for winning or losing.*
>
> *Either way, you're all in it together."*

NO PLAYING ON THE BATTLEFIELD

The battlefield reflects the precise teamwork that is expected on the playing field. But you're not playing on that field. It's not a game. When someone doesn't execute their requisite task, people can die.

"If one person couldn't hack it, we all failed.
That's the true essence of teamwork."

As a SOAR member, I was among a team of soldiers responsible for extracting or inserting the Quick Response Force (QRF). In other words, we dropped them into their mission area and picked them up after they completed it. These covert missions were always executed at night. The Regiment had a motto: NSDQ—Night Stalkers Don't Quit. Anything less than 100% success was a failure. If one person couldn't hack it, we all failed. That's the true essence of teamwork.

As they say, there is no "I" in "TEAM".

FIGHTING FOR YOUR TEAM

One of the most powerful examples of a motivated team spanned two continents. My fellow West Point alum and true badass, Jim Young, joined a group of former service people, led by David Abrams, set out on a unique mission to aid their Afghan counterparts escape the Taliban. Abrams is a former Infantry Colonel who served as a military governor in western Afghanistan on his last tour of duty. In addition to his other duties, David interacted with the tribal leaders.

In August 2021, David learned that many former Afghanistan combat interpreters, allies, and soldiers were trying desperately to evacuate the country after Americans were pulled out. These allies faced mountains of paperwork to gain approval to flee their country. The possibility of freedom seemed hopeless.

David assembled a team of Army veterans to process the complex network of paperwork required by the State Department and other government agencies. Because of the time difference between the United States and Afghanistan, where the refugees waited, the Americans worked night after night. As they tirelessly completed the forms, 37,000 people were stranded outside the Hamid Karzai International Airport in Kabul without food and water, while enduring temperatures of 113 degrees.

"What we've been doing is paperwork, documents, trying to coordinate the massive amounts of information that these different departments want these evacuees to try and put together while they're fleeing. It's extremely difficult. And so, from here in the United States, we're able to coordinate with laptops and Salesforce and encrypted apps to put these things together, submit them, and if they want changes, to resubmit them," Jim said.

The volunteers were recruited on private message boards, using covert methods, like wiping cell phones, to protect the evacuees from being discovered by the Taliban, who were taking over cell phone towers.

Days and days of calls might result in a one lucky break with someone getting moved into the airport. Once inside, however, these evacuees faced more challenges. They could endure many more days to get through the biometric system to get close to the terminal's gates and one step closer to safety.

The group of veteran volunteers, under the name "Task Force Grip Hands" grew to 50 people. Jim said the team became more sophisticated, forming committees and getting support from two senators, three congressmen, a former Secretary of State, and the governor of Texas.

Despite countless hours of efforts by these dedicated veterans, the progress was slow.

"Occasionally, we'd get a photo text of a very happy family sitting on a tarmac who had flown out and was safe in a processing center," Jim said.

Task Force Grip Hands learned of a former combat interpreter who was living in Austin. He had earned U.S. citizenship as a result of serving seven years in combat with American soldiers- -four more years than was required. Unfortunately, families were not granted the same privilege. "Henry", who used this false name to protect his family in Afghanistan, served four years with the Army and three years with the Marines in Afghanistan. During a three-day battle, his Marine unit was trapped in a valley where they were surrounded by 1,400 Taliban fighters. The Taliban leaders offered all interpreters the chance to walk out freely. Henry and his compatriots stayed and continued the fight alongside the American troops.

When Jim, David, and their team heard that Henry's family had failed numerous times to escape Afghanistan, they stepped in. Their research found out about planes being chartered to fly people out of Afghanistan. The group met someone who had chartered a plane, and they became hopeful. But one of the donors pulled out and the flight was on hold. The task force launched a campaign and raised the money needed for the charter. When flight clearance was finally issued, the family had just one hour to get to the transport that would take them to the airport. A few tense hours later, Jim and his colleagues received word that the plane carrying Henry's family had cleared Afghanistan air space. They were on their way to reunite in Austin, Texas.

Jim says he and his colleagues spoke often about why they gave so much effort to this cause. "All this time, our wives and kids were wondering why we weren't making it to soccer games and family events or why I was routinely falling asleep at family events.

"I see myself in him. I was in the Army for eight years and I see a man just like me. And honestly, it really hurts me that someone who spent seven years fighting with my friends, translating for them, protecting their lives, shouldn't have to ask for favors for his wife and children to pass through a gate," he said.

"We learned our guidepost words of Duty, Honor, Country were not just words. They were standards we could hold onto when we were exhausted."

When you're part of a team, you don't ask "Why?" You already know the reason you do what you do.

BUILD YOUR TEAM, ONE AT A TIME

You know the importance of a team. Now, let's look at bringing the right people to your team. Remember, one bad apple sours the whole bushel.

Golf is an individual sport so it might seem strange to use it as an example in team-building, but bear with me on this.

Golf has been a big part of my life since I was a teenager. I love competing against myself, to achieve my personal best. With each game, I find new ways to improve. It's also an activity my wife, Chris, and I have enjoyed together—just about every weekend—since the early days of our relationship. When we moved to Austin, Chris joined a women's league. She developed a friendship with Pearl Fields, a fascinating and insightful person. Pearl also happens to be married to Coach John Fields, the head of the University of Texas men's golf team since 1997—and one of the winningest golf coaches of all time.

As Chris and Pearl became friends, they decided that their husbands needed to meet. I was honored to meet Coach Fields and even more excited to build a friendship with him. He possesses an innate ability to identify talent in young people. Under Coach Fields's leadership, the UT men's golf team won a national championship and posted 65 tournament victories. That achievement is the result of strong teamwork, which results from choosing strong players.

Coach knows what to look for in a prospect as far as the skill set, desire, and trainability. For the rest, his wife of 40 years partners with Coach to evaluate candidates. The team's alumni include such notable players as Jordan Spieth, a member of the 2012 NCAA Championship Team. He went on to win his first Masters at the age of 21 and the U.S. Open Championship at 23. Scottie Scheffler, another pro who was guided by Coach John Fields, won the 2022 Arnold Palmer Invitational, his first PGA Tour win.

In addition to Jordan and Scottie, other current PGA golfers who were coached by John Fields include Brad Elder, David Gossett, Tim Herron, Kent Jones, Sean Murphy, and Dylan Fritelli.

For every team member, the University commits to a golf scholarship for the full four years of their education. It's an investment they don't enter into lightly, just like hiring a person. If that player doesn't help the team, they've taken the place of someone who might have been better, so it's a very careful decision. Coach, who twice earned Coach of the Year from the Golf Coaches Association

> **There is no way around the work ethic.**
>
> —Coach John Fields

of America, looks at the skills and trainability of a young man.

"There is no way around the work ethic," explained Coach. "They need to work hard and be motivated."

Pearl assesses the character of the high school students they're considering for a spot on the 10- to 13-person team.

"You watch how they carry themselves. You can see that from a distance," Pearl says. "The parents matter more than anything. Are they too involved, not involved enough? One boy's dad wanted him to play golf so badly, but his son got to college and didn't want to play; he wanted to go to school. Becoming a pro golfer was his dad's dream, not his. Coach helped him with his degree and his career, and the young man was happy, but the father blamed John that his son didn't become a professional. We love the parents, but we don't serve the parents. It's about the kids, not the parents. They have to be able to help the team, in the classroom or on the golf course."

Coach enters five players in each golf tournament. The top four scores are added together for the team's total. There's a very small margin for error in that set-up. One player can falter, and his teammates carry him through. But if two of them have a bad day on the course, the whole team fails.

Does this sound familiar? Have you or your team's leader brought in someone who just didn't mesh with the rest of the team? What was the long-term result? If that weak link isn't removed, it impedes the workflow of everyone else.

SEEK URGENCY

When I was transitioning out of the military and into civilian life, I reconnected with a former Blackhawk pilot. Like me, Jeff Jepson had flown helicopters for seven years and went on to build a successful career in resort properties and commercial real estate. Jeff has always relied on his military training to assess situations and people.

"My military training instilled in me the idea of teamwork. It inspired my way of looking at business," Jeff told me. "I don't recruit a group of individuals to sell real estate. We build teams."

"When we hire employees, a predictor of success is their urgency, similar to accountability. I want to gauge the pace at which people process and execute their work." The construction company Jeff manages is guided by timelines and penalties, putting more pressure on players to perform at their peak. "We can't have an average player show up on the team. You need a high level of urgency. That means you don't write a thirty-minute email when you can do a three-minute email."

> *"I don't recruit a group of individuals.*
> *We build teams."*
>
> —Jeff Jepson, former Blackhawk pilot

SEEING RED

I learned valuable lessons about building a team from some impressive people—badasses, all of them. A few years back, the company I had started, Legacy International Resort Properties, had expanded to the point where I knew I needed another person on the leadership team. I couldn't keep my eye on guiding the growth while also overseeing everyday activities. Chris and I talked about the type of person and qualities we needed for this role. We decided on a Chief Operating Officer. Chris had someone specific in mind: Mandy Van Streepen, a sharp, savvy badass who was already on our payroll, but currently doled out to one of the most successful and inspiring people I've ever known: Red McCombs.

I had originally recruited Mandy in 2015, for a Legacy International role with the sales and marketing leadership team that was managing a portfolio of resort properties for Red. He is an intuitive, gutsy entrepreneur who is masterful at team-building. To appreciate the depth of the responsibility that Mandy was tasked with, I need to give you some highlights of Red McCombs' achievements so you can begin to gauge the level of expectations.

First of all, if you don't recognize the name, you're not a Texan.

An entrepreneur with gargantuan successes, Red built an auto dealership empire, Red McCombs Automotive Group. He went on to co-found Clear Channel Communications, a mass media company that began in 1972 with his partner, Lowry Mays and their purchase of a San Antonio FM radio station. The two men went on to acquire more stations, accumulating 43 radio stations and 16 television stations by 1995. It evolved with the digital age and continued steady expansion. Red and Lowry sold Clear Channel in 2008. Now known as iHeartMedia, Inc., the company posts an annual revenue of more than $3.6 billion.

Red, a diehard San Antonian and lifelong entrepreneur, used his considerable skills, knowledge, and wealth to purchase the San Antonio Spurs of the NBA. He later sold the franchise and acquired the Denver Nuggets.

In 1993, after selling the Spurs, Red turned his attention to professional football. He wanted to bring an NFL franchise to San Antonio. In his autobiography, *"Big Red: Memoirs of a Texas Entrepreneur and Philanthropist"*, Red said "I briefly toyed with the idea of buying the New England Patriots, but that deal had too many legal entanglements."[1]

He worked tirelessly toward his goal. In 1998, Red purchased the Minnesota Vikings. Despite his desire to establish an NFL team in San Antonio, Red knew that he needed to keep the Vikings in Minnesota.

Not only did he keep them in their hometown of Minneapolis, but Red also built a new stadium for the team. He was certain that they had the talent to do better with the right leadership. When Red learned that the Vikings had never sold-out tickets for the exhibition games held just prior the season, he chided his staff, saying "Kids in the street play exhibition games." He then pronounced "The Vikings play preseason games, and I don't ever want to hear that other word again."

---

1 McCombs, Red, and Don Carleton, 2011, *Big Red: Memoirs of a Texas Entrepreneur and Philanthropist*, Dolph Briscoe Center for American History at the University of Texas at Austin, page 164

Red also recognized that he needed to keep his coach focused on a winning season and not his contract, which was in its final year. He gave Coach Dennis Green a three-year extension and substantial raise. And all talk of "what if" regarding the coach's future with the team was silenced. Instead, Coach Green and his players set to work on doing their jobs.

Red was a master of motivating teams. In 1998, with a new stadium and a coach with a long-term commitment, the team achieved a 15-1 record. In the Vikings' history, the 1998-99 season is recognized as one of the top five they ever had, and they have not beaten that record since then. Then again, the only thing better than 15-1 in football is 16-0, a perfect season that would then be capped off with a Super Bowl victory.

The consummate entrepreneur, Red McCombs expanded his interest and built a portfolio of resort properties. And that's where Mandy Van Streepen comes in.

RIDING THE ENERGY BUS

Mandy Van Streepen is one of the best recruiters I've known. I watched her masterfully navigate the sales and marketing operations for Red McCombs properties. She operated within a team of motivated, results-driven professionals who consistently exceeded expectations—mine and, more importantly, those of Red and his leadership group. In 2017, Mandy had transitioned from being on loan to McCombs Properties to working directly for them, at their request. Keeping Red McCombs happy was a priority for me, so I signed off on that switch.

As I mentioned, when Chris and I were pondering the position of Chief Operating Officer for Legacy International in August of 2018, we discussed the qualities and experience that the ideal candidate would have.

Chris possesses the enviable and innate ability to read people. She is like the perfect complement that Pearl Fields is to Coach John Fields. I respect her perspective because it's almost always spot on.

Chris said, "What about Mandy?"

"**Energy vampires are the toxic riders on the bus who need to be dropped off at the next stop.**"

I looked at her for a moment, wordlessly processing the idea, and responded simply, "Damn."

With very little discussion, I reached out to Mandy and invited her to meet me at a restaurant for a conversation. We talked about the need for a COO at Legacy International and I extended her a job offer. I remember writing the offer on a napkin and sliding it across the table. She accepted. Two months later, Mandy was back in Legacy International headquarters.

As Chief Operating Officer of Legacy International, Mandy oversees the operation of an international company. Still, the core team at the headquarters is relatively small. She has no room for "bad apples" on the team.

Mandy calls her approach to hiring "The Energy Bus", inspired by the book of the same name_by Jon Gordon. It's a vehicle in motion that operates on positive energy.

"I need to put the right people in the right seats at the right time. If I have one person who goes wonky, it upsets the whole team. One wrong move can upset the momentum of what we've established."

In his book, Gordon describes "energy vampires". These negative individuals drain you of energy and cause you to detour from your goals and vision. They are the toxic riders on the bus who need to be dropped off at the next stop. I told you that Mandy is a master recruiter, a perceptive visionary of talent.

When she evaluates candidates for a position on the team, Mandy doesn't rely on the resume. "My job is to establish if they are the right fit. I look at their values, their goals, their vision, and whether they can pull up their sleeves and get the job done. Everybody pitches in. I cannot afford to have someone who has an ego. That goes against everything we stand for."

When she interviews sales professionals, Mandy asks them, "What is your favorite movie and why should I watch it?"

She isn't looking for movie recommendations. She is seeking a glimpse at their approach to selling. Mandy is also determining whether they have the all-important, innate ability to get to the customer's "why".

"If that person just tells me about their favorite movie, they've missed an important point. What kind of movies do I like? They need to qualify me first. If they don't, I see their weakness as a salesperson."

Mandy came to the United States from South Africa seven years earlier. Here's a little background on her own "Why".

She and her husband were raising two daughters in a country where the crime rate is staggering. Violence was quite literally outside their door, even though they lived in an upscale residential neighborhood. Neighbors were carjacked right in front of the Van Streepens' home, at gunpoint and in broad daylight. She and her husband decided to leave their homeland in search of a safer life for their family. They decided on the United States. The Van Streepens eventually found their way to Austin, and a fellow South African working for me recruited Mandy.

In less than five years, she has built some of the strongest teams I've ever seen. And I'm not talking about sales figures. They possess passion in unlimited amounts. I saw it in the aftermath of Hurricane Harvey's destruction along the Texas Coast. These professionals rolled up their sleeves and put their job titles aside. Mandy was put in charge of communication with the homeowners, buyers, and HOA members in two of the McCombs communities. She led groups of their team, loading up vans with supplies in Austin and taking them to the Coast where people didn't even have drinking water. Mandy and her crew of 10 people at any given time camped out in one, three-bedroom condominium, taking turns sleeping while others met the needs of the people who had been ravaged by the storm.

"There wasn't a moment of hesitation," Mandy recalls when she recruited their help. "They were galvanized. And that community came out of this horrific disaster because of that early response."

DEHIRING, NOT FIRING

Managing a team is a demanding task in various ways. Cutting a teammate can be necessary for the well-being of the group, but it's not a pleasant chore. No one likes to fire someone. Some of us see a person who has a family, plans for the future, and relies on this job and the paycheck that goes with it. But when you keep someone who isn't pulling their weight, what message does it send to the other people on the team?

The hard-working individuals are probably working even harder to make up for the slacker. Is that fair to them? And what are they sacrificing in return? Maybe those who are pitching in and doing extra aren't able to achieve their goals or their work isn't the high quality you expect. So, by keeping that weak link, you're putting strain on them and compromising the results.

You're also sending out a message that it's ok to be mediocre in this group. Do you really want to set mediocrity as an acceptable standard? By doing so, you risk having your best people move on to a less dysfunctional group.

My mentor, Myers Barnes, advised me that, in reality, you don't fire people. They dehire themselves. You've explained the job and your expectations of their performance. When they fail to live up to it, they've made the choice to NOT fulfill the duties. It's their actions that prompt your reaction. With this advice, Myers, a new home sales trainer and author of numerous books on the subject, shifted the responsibility to where it belongs—the employee.

> *"In reality, you don't fire people.*
>
> *They de-hire themselves.*
>
> *They've made the choice to*
> *NOT fulfill the duties of their job."*
>
> —Myers Barnes

It doesn't end with the singular act of termination. As these under-performers make the choice to dehire themselves, you have leadership responsibility. You can merely sever ties and wish them well, or you can demonstrate a powerful aspect of emotional intel-

"Do you want to set mediocrity as an acceptable standard?"

ligence: empathy. Help the departing employee understand their poor fit with your company, identify a path to something more suitable. You certainly don't need to hunt around for a job, but you can give them direction.

Does this sound like your team? Are you ready to make the tough decisions to protect the strength of your team?

T-E-A-M

I believe in the power of teamwork. Whether the team is my wife and daughters, my colleagues at Legacy International and Legacy Performance Capital, my strategic partnerships, the tenured relationships, my church, or my close friends, I know I can rely on each group to work side by side with me. They are part of me, and I am part of them.

That's what you should always expect of your teams and teammates. When you lower those expectations, you weaken the team.

We're setting out to lead with a Life Equation in this book. It starts and ends with the caliber of the team. I learned team building from various aspects—on the football field, in the military, and nearly two decades of building the Legacy enterprise.

> ### *"When you lower expectations, you weaken the team."*

Every decision, every action had to be measured against how it fit into my formula. I knew my "Why." I lived it. And whenever there was temptation to take a detour, I was lucky enough to have people step in, like my dad who reminded me why I wanted to go to West Point when I was ready to walk away. I've had the family of Special Operators who would give their lives to protect mine, as I would do for them. And I've been blessed with the badasses in my career who inspire me to be a strong leader, to never give up, because that's the easiest thing to do, but not the right thing.

LIFE EQUATION LESSON

A team can be as small as two people. The purpose is to band together for a common purpose. Every relationship makes you part of a team—your life partner, friends, family, co-workers, and members of organizations, clubs, and groups. Know your teams, your role, and why they matter, because the influence in your life is more powerful than you may realize.

FACTOR IN YOUR ANSWERS

1. *Thinking about the various teams that you've been a member of, which ones have made the biggest difference in your life? Why?*

2. *What qualities do you think are essential to be a good team member?*

3. *If you could reorganize the roster on one of your teams to make it stronger, what changes would you make and why? How could you strengthen certain players rather than replace them?*

4. *Do you have "energy vampires" in your life? Who are they and what are those relationships costing you?*

+ CHAPTER 5

CHANGE, CHOICE, AND CHANCE

Change is one of those things that you either love or hate—like lima beans and the New York Yankees.

Change is scary to some people and exciting to others. Regardless of how you feel about change, it's inevitable. So, you should learn how to deal with it. Grumbling or ignoring the situation won't help.

Why do we need to embrace change? How does it fit into a Life Equation?

BIG FISH + SMALL POND = BIG DREAMS

I had my whole life planned out when I was 16. I would play football for the rest of my high school career (offensive tight end). I would go on to the United States Military Academy at West Point and then serve in the Army. And I figured I'd be an officer.

I can't say my desire to go to West Point was based on any noble purpose, other than to be part of something bigger. As a teenager, I have to admit I had very little knowledge about what a good leader really was. I was enticed by the challenge—both to get accepted and then to complete the rigorous four-year program. In truth, "rigorous" doesn't begin to convey the pain, stress, and intimidation that's rolled up into a West Point education, but, for now, we'll leave it at that.

My best friend's older brother was already attending West Point. He regaled us with stories about getting your head shaved on day one, taking verbal beatings from upperclassmen, and workouts that made my football workouts on hot summer days in full gear seem like a day at the beach.

My buddy, Greg Anderson, was planning on following in his brother's footsteps and going to West Point. I wasn't fazed by the statistic that there are 14,000 applicants for only 1,200 slots. In fact, that challenge enticed me. Only a few people in my family had attended college, let alone West Point. I always liked proving that I could do what others told me I could not achieve.

So, West Point sounded like a good idea to me, certainly something more unique than a conventional college experience. As a football player in a Texas high school, I was a fairly big fish in a fairly small pond, so I felt confident about getting into West Point.

Then I ended up wedged under a car seat in a car that was dangling from a tree.

A CHANGE FOR THE BETTER?

The car accident in 1987, right before senior year, didn't just change the well-laid plans for my future. The injury sent my dream careening off its path with the same velocity as that car when it hurled off the road and into the tree.

I just didn't know it at the time.

Colliding with that tree in 1987 was an accident. But it started me on a path filled with purpose. And I learned the value of navigating through changes, something that would serve me well throughout my life!

"You don't have to take huge leaps of change.

Baby steps will do."

CHOOSING CHANGE

Change is inevitable. Every situation is temporary. The Earth keeps rotating. No day is exactly the same as the one before. Our bodies change with time. And time passes. Clinging to the past or the present prevents you from exploring the possibilities that the future holds.

Change is also part of growth—growing your knowledge, your experience, and your network. You will never go beyond your current place if you don't step outside your comfort zone once in a while. Explore the possibilities. You don't need to take huge leaps to change. Baby steps will do.

An important step in feeling comfortable with change is establishing a process for choosing it.

There are lots of ways to make a decision that brings about a change of some kind. You can make a list of pros and cons to weigh the two sides against each other. You can flip a coin—although I wouldn't recommend it unless you truly don't care which choice to take.

You can also survey other people. I think we've all done this, but, from my experience, you need to filter whom you ask. Some people will tell you what they think you want to hear, and that's not helpful. In other cases, the individuals you talk to are putting their own personal bias and experience into a decision. Your life isn't theirs. Unless the decision you make impacts them, I suggest you steer away from "decision by committee". Respect your unique perspective. Slow down long enough to make sure you are looking at the situation through your own lens. Trust me, it matters.

Personally, I think when you ask around for other people's opinions on your choice, you're probably looking for them to affirm the way you're already leaning. Or it's a matter of having them eliminate the guilt you're feeling about choosing one side over another. For example, you're trying to decide whether to attend your in-laws' family party or go to a pro football game using the tickets you just scored for free. You want to go to the game, but you also want to appease the family. You're hoping that the people you ask will lessen your guilt about skipping the in-laws' party, right? Do you survey just your football-loving buddies or ask around through the family network?

Ultimately, the decision you make will be yours to live with.

LIFE = (CHOICE + CHOICE)^n

Your life is the sum of your choices—good and bad, right and wrong, and everywhere in between.

Go back to a decision you made at least a few years ago. It could be deciding to go to a place where you ended up meeting your significant other. Maybe it's the decision you made to choose (or not choose) a job. You could look at the decision you made of where to live or with whom.

> *"Your life is the sum of your choices—good and bad, right and wrong, and everywhere in between."*

Now ask yourself, "What would have happened if I took another path? Where might that have led me?" Follow the branches. Explore the possibilities.

What if John F. Kennedy decided not to go to Dallas in November 1963? He would not have been assassinated that day. Lyndon Johnson might not have become President and the chain of U.S. Presidents we've had since 1963 would undoubtedly be quite different.

If Kennedy survived his term and even had a second one, the Vietnam War could have ended differently. What would that have meant to the soldiers serving there? How many would have lived or died because Kennedy stayed in office?

Spend some time doing a "What if...?" exercise and you'll see how even a seemingly minor choice can totally change your life. Don't let someone else make decisions for you. Remember that even when you don't make a choice, that's a choice. You're picking inaction. Is that really what you want?

"Even when you don't make a choice, that's a choice."

LIFE EQUATION LESSON

Change happens. You can flow it, ride atop the wave, or sink. Learn to navigate change by being agile, finding your way to harness the benefits, overcome the challenges, and grow from it.

FACTOR IN YOUR ANSWERS

1. *How do you handle change? Do you welcome it, resist it, or somewhere in between?*

2. *What impacts the way you respond to change?*

3. *What is a change in your life that was difficult to adapt to? Why?*

4. *Is there a change you wish you had made but didn't? What influenced your decision? Knowing what you know now, what might have happened if you chose differently?*

+ CHAPTER 6

THE ROAD TO AND THROUGH WEST POINT

What choices have you made today? What consequences can you expect? Some have a major impact on our lives, and others, not so much. When you're making a decision, do you know which way your choice will guide you? A chance encounter can turn into a life-changer. Maybe it's whether you go to college. Or it could be the career path you pick, or the one you leave behind in favor of a new direction.

A Life Equation is a measuring stick that helps with decision-making. As you weigh your options, figure out how one choice or the other supports your core values and your life plan. It might sound calculating, but isn't that better than leaving it all up to chance?

By now, you know that getting to West Point was a major goal for me. As a kid from a small town with very limited experience, I didn't think through the process of getting THROUGH West Point. I just assumed I would.

I learned a lot of lessons during those four years that contributed to factors in my Life Equation: teamwork, training, strategy, and accountability. That's a lot to learn! I want to share how this experience guides a young person into adulthood with mission-critical values, like integrity and accountability. Those values added so much to my own Life Equation and my intent here is to illustrate how experiences and choices go hand in hand.

GRAB AN IDEA AND HANG ON TIGHT

Some people, like me, get an idea in their head and go after it with bull-headed relentlessness. When that full-powered pursuit is fueled by passion, you're heading in the right direction. Pure unadulterated stubbornness, however, is another story. Be mindful of your motivation and be prepared to adjust your action plans if you're veering off track.

> *"When full-powered pursuit is fueled by passion, you're heading in the right direction.*
>
> *Pure, unadulterated stubbornness is another story."*

When I first entertained the thought of attending West Point, I admit that I was imagining myself in the crisp white uniform, marching in perfect unison with my fellow cadets.

I didn't picture the grueling workouts, the long hours spent studying, and the strict set of rules that impacted every activity—days, nights, and weekends. Never did I think about marching for hours in the freezing cold for punishment that arose from one stupid choice, which I'll share later.

A PURPOSEFUL CHOICE

Not every high school student wants a conventional route beyond high school. Some head right into their career. Others pursue travel, taking time to "find" themselves. I didn't have the luxury to go wandering to find myself. From my small Texas hometown,

I just thought deeply and carefully about what I wanted in my life. Conventional higher education definitely wasn't it. In high school, I thrived on challenges. Tell me I can't do something and watch me dig in my heels and get it done. I wanted something big—bigger than a normal state university.

It was clear that the U.S. Military Academy at West Point would give me much more than a college degree, as long as I put in the work—something that was never a problem. If you talk to any West Point alum, you'll hear the common theme that they wanted something different when they chose to seek a nomination to the Academy. They sought a bigger challenge, a pathway to military leadership, or the nobility of purpose.

Jim Young, a West Point classmate of mine, said he chose West Point because he wanted "to be someone and do something great." But he also says his incentive was fired up by stories like my own excitement that grew from listening to the tales of my friend's older brother.

Jim's dad was in the Army. As a teenager, Jim mowed lawns on the military base where they lived. One of his customers was a colonel. He once invited Jim into the house where a shining saber mounted on the wall captured Jim's attention. Seeing the boy's amazement, the colonel told him it was his West Point saber. In that instant, Jim knew he wanted a saber like that.

"They tell you not to go to West Point because you want some sort of image, but I wanted to do something unique and special and hard. I knew that signing up was something honest, which made me proud." For Jim, that saber symbolized a meaningful "something".

Getting into West Point took extra effort for him. When he first applied to the Academy, Jim was told his grades weren't good enough. Faced with that obstacle, he didn't give up, as many others his age might have. Instead, he sought alternative paths. He found a delayed entry program that allowed him to enlist at age 17 and go to basic training in the summer between his junior and senior years of high school. After finishing basic training in high school, Jim went to his West Point interview and told them he had already joined the

"Those who give up will never know how close they came to succeeding."

Army. He said he wanted the Academy's training so he could be ready for the job. He was accepted in April of his senior year.

Jim Young didn't take "no" for an answer because passion pushed him to keep going after his goal. Have you ever hit an obstacle and then found an alternate route to your destination? Imagine if you hadn't done that. Those who give up will never know how close they came to succeeding.

Jim and I continue to lean on one another, sharing strategy about real estate projects. We have a solid relationship built on the trust that comes from having shared a leadership training experience. We know what we can expect from one another, because we know we started our careers from an identical entry point. Shared experience provides a valuable bond when it comes with shared learning and application of those experiences.

A LEAP OF FAITH

Another West Point classmate of mine, Harry Adams, said he chose the Academy because he aspired to "go someplace that meant something."

Harry had been invited to a West Point Recruiting Fair in his hometown of San Antonio during the summer before his senior year in high school. He recalls it was an impressive presentation, but one thing really stood out in his mind: "The cadets—six feet tall, big jaws and shoulders, and the crisp uniform."

He also had another scenario for his future—to be a surfer in California. Probably as far from being a West Point Cadet as anyone could imagine.

Harry had considered Ivy League schools, along with UCLA and Texas. He visited UCLA and Berkeley with his mother. He was able to see Ziggy Marley performing live on the Berkeley campus. For someone who had dreams of being a California surfer, this seemed like the right place.

But the experience had the opposite effect on Harry.

"I had a great time but the next morning, I told my mom it

wasn't the right place for me. I realized I didn't want that kind of college experience."

Harry and his mom returned to San Antonio, satisfied that he had gained the clarity he needed. Harry went through the West Point nomination appointment process without ever visiting the campus. The day he reported to West Point was the first time he saw it in person.

He took the leap of faith fully confident that it was the right thing to do. Harry felt the passion in his heart and soul, signs that he made the right decision. He admits there were times over the next four years when he questioned his choice, but they were moments when he was facing a tough challenge. In each instance, Harry rose up and became stronger, a powerful benefit of not giving into something that's harder than you expected.

Harry and I are now strategic partners, both managing substantial real estate portfolios. We count on each other to live up to commitments, to be honest when things are not what we hoped, and to treat each other with respect, no matter what. Academy alums know what the West Point education delivers. Beyond academics, it's integrity, leadership, and commitment.

DO MORE THAN YOU THINK YOU CAN

No matter where you go to continue your education—from trade school to university—you expect to work harder than you have done to that point in your life. You take it for granted that you'll have to adapt to a new way of life. But the naïveté of a 17-year-old from a small Texas town soon discovered that military college was more than I expected.

It might be hard to fathom why someone would choose such a demanding college experience when there are plenty of colleges and universities where you can enjoy more freedom and fun—like seeing Ziggy Marley at Berkeley. If you have the forethought at a young age to map out your life, at least for the foreseeable future, you can prioritize your life choices. There will always be time for fun. And never forget that "fun" comes in many forms.

*"A powerful sense of honor, duty, and pride
hangs in the air at West Point."*

When life (and the car accident) happened, I took a detour from my planned path to West Point, going via Marion Military Institute instead. As a junior military college, the school wasn't a cake walk. The academics and the daily routine presented big challenges, starting with Advanced ROTC training camp the summer before my freshman year. College football was tougher than high school. A lot tougher. There were times right from the start that I questioned my decision but pressed on to maintain the strength of my commitment. And when I faltered, my dad reminded me of that same choice.

Like Harry, I had to make a leap of faith when choosing West Point. I willingly gave up my officer's commission from Marion Military Institute to push forward on my dream of attending the Academy. I had to start over, as a first-year, in spite of having completed two years at Marion. I have never regretted the decision. In fact, it was without a doubt one of the best choices I've made in my life. I invested four more years of my life in my future, training with some of the most inspiring, knowledgeable leaders around. I even had the chance to spend a summer interning at the Center for Strategic and International Studies, a policy think tank for national security. I worked for the most renowned expert on North Korea. He charged me—an intern!—with reviewing and analyzing key data. I carefully studied and reported on the resources that were being allocated to the military to accomplish two major and one limited conflict at the same time. We were trying to answer the question, "Was our country equipped to handle numerous conflicts at once?" My report would influence national policy, eventually forming an argument that would become a thesis.

And it began with a leap of faith to Marion Military Institute that landed me at West Point.

THE TOUGH GET TOUGHER

By the time I stepped onto the West Point campus as an incoming cadet—who was two years older than the other plebes—I was far more prepared than the Mama's boy who left Tomball, Texas, for Marion Military Institute.

A powerful sense of honor, duty, and pride hangs in the air at West Point—not overpowering, but a steady reminder that you're part of something so much larger than yourself.

Designated a National Historic Landmark in 1960, West Point's history is evident in every corner. There's a saying that is often used at West Point, "The history we teach was made by many of the people we taught."

You can't help but feel honored when you're walking on the grounds once occupied by history-makers like Ulysses S. Grant, Dwight D. Eisenhower, George Custer, Stonewall Jackson, George S. Patton, Robert E. Lee, Buzz Aldrin, Douglas MacArthur, and Norman Schwarzkopf, just to name a few. People who have gone above and beyond. Sharing that heritage excites and inspires you to maintain that strength of character, to do something bigger than yourself.

West Point trains leaders—people who will be responsible for the lives and actions of others—with the mission, "Duty, Honor, Country". They will lead in the military and the civilian world. The educators and leaders at West Point are laser focused on instilling values to steer a person to tackle a life with integrity. The experience empowers you with a sense of purpose, dedication, and honor.

DAY ONE OF A NEW LIFE

The difference between a military academy and conventional education is crystal clear from day one. Incoming cadets report to West Point in June so they can spend the summer training before the fall semester. Reception Day—known as "R-Day"—gives cadets and their families a startling transition from civilian to military academy life. It's a day every cadet remembers.

On R-Day, you report early and are given a time to show up in the athletic stadium. The cadets gather on the field while their parents are seated in the stands. A cadet welcomes you, you say your good-byes to your family, and everyone files out.

So far, not much notable, right? Just wait.

Without mom and dad, you're on your own in an environment that's so far from anything you've encountered. You go from being a carefree high school kid to military life in one day. You're pushed through a series of activities and tests that come at you at a mind-numbing pace.

Once you leave the parade field, you're instructed to put your personal belongings in a bag, and you're issued clothes to wear for the day (black shirt, shorts, socks, and shoes). You're assigned to your barracks, which are known as "Beast Barracks" for first-years or "plebes". You're given a set of tags, with each one representing a different station where you will report throughout the day. At each station, a senior cadet—the "Man in the Red Sash"—looks at your ticket and sends you to your next station when you've finished whatever it is you've been directed to do. You get your head shaved, get measured for your uniform, go through a physical assessment, and complete about 20 other tasks.

On R-Day, you are taught the correct way to stand, march, and salute. You're given a copy of "Bugle Notes", essentially a cadet handbook that explains the purpose and process of West Point's standards and activities. This book teaches you everything from the Honor Code to how to address an upperclassman. Plebes are expected to memorize everything contained in Bugle Notes, and you WILL be tested continually. Failure to respond with the correct knowledge will earn you grueling chores that will "encourage" you to put more effort into memorizing every single paragraph in Bugle Notes.

Throughout R-Day, you're also verbally, mentally, and physically hazed by upperclassmen. All. Day. Long.

At the end of the day, the new cadets return to the parade field. They march for the first time as a group in front of the spectators, including parents who are bursting with pride, totally unaware of what their kids have just endured to get to this moment. After dinner, the cadets go to their rooms, armed with duties to be completed before lights out.

Let me give you a closer look at R-Day, courtesy of my class-mate, Harry Adams.

> *"An upperclassman kicked the trash can across the room.*
>
> *Across the campus, the loudspeakers blared the song, 'Welcome to the Jungle'."*

"I remember lying in bed after lights went out, looking up at the ceiling, and wondering, what the hell did I do? The next morn-ing, I awoke to a crashing sound. There was a government-issued, metal trash can that propped the door open all night. Early that morning, an upperclassman kicked the trash can across the room. Across the campus, the loudspeakers blared the song, 'Welcome to the Jungle'."

That's how it starts. As you can imagine, this life isn't for every cadet. Approximately 1,300 cadets make it through the grueling appointment process and enroll at West Point (chosen from about 4,000 applicants). About 900 to 1,000 actually graduate. My class lost 400 cadets over the four years. For those of us who stayed, the leadership training and the experiences that were part of it deliv-ered a lifelong volume of invaluable lessons.

EXTRAORDINARY MENTORS

Here's what sets a West Point education apart from a conven-tional one. Imagine being a pre-med student and having the oppor-tunity to spend an entire summer as an undergraduate watching surgeries in the operating rooms at Walter Reed Hospital.

Think about what it would be like as a pre-law student to intern at the Pentagon or to have lunch with Supreme Court justices.

As I mentioned, I worked with some of the smartest minds at the Center for Strategic and International Studies. As a student major-ing in Economics and Political Science, picture the awe-inspiring

> ## I felt like I was living in a history book sometimes.

—Jim Young, West Point alumnus

experience of watching strategic superminds develop policies that could determine the outcome of future battles and even impact global decisions.

West Point gives its cadets the benefit of knowledge from a vast array of experts. General Norman Schwarzkopf, a West Point alum, visited the campus shortly after returning from leading Americans to success in Operation Desert Storm.

Dr. Edward Teller was known as "the father of the hydrogen bomb" and a member of the infamous Manhattan Project. He was also a visiting professor of Physics at West Point. Dr. Teller described to his students the difficulty of the decision of how to use nuclear fusion and the ethics of creating a bomb that could destroy massive populations.

These are the kinds of opportunities, conversations, and engagements that West Point cadets experience. Mentorship of this caliber was not lost on us. We knew that our choice had brought us to that "something bigger, different, and better."

Jim Young looks back at those four years with appreciation for what he was given. "I remember when we were flying in helicopters over the Hudson River or rappelling off rocks, 'this is so much better than being at a keg party!' You could grab a friend and go running up a mountain or shoot M16s at a range, things a college student would never do."

During his internship prior to senior year, Jim, a pre-law major, attended congressional hearings. His job was to report legal arguments that might affect the military. He wrote a briefing after one hearing and was excited when the Chairman of the Joint Chiefs of Staff used part of Jim's briefing during an interview on "60 Minutes".

Three weeks later, Jim was in Germany where he was assigned to a tank unit to do gunnery exercises.

"Any normal college experience could never hold a candle to that," Jim says, still exuberant over the opportunity given to him by the "The Great American Public" who paid for his education. "I had classmates who went on to become generals and experience the heat of battle. I felt like I was living in a history book sometimes."

POWER LIFTING AND THE PINK THONG

These activities inspired cadets to work harder. Each one had their own motivators. It's different for everyone, but Harry Adams learned something about motivation at West Point.

The cadet gymnasium is something to behold. The massive structure is four stories tall and houses basketball courts, pools, boxing rings, and fitness areas. Harry had a friend, Eric, who was on the power lifting team, and who just so happened to be both my roommate and power lifting teammate. Eric invited Harry to work out with him.

Harry and Eric headed downstairs to the power lifting training room. They went even lower than the basement, to the sub-basement. At the bottom of the stairs, there's a small space and a door lit by a single bulb. On the door, there's a drawing of a character who is half-person, half-beast. It's accompanied by the words "Animal House" painted in a Metallica-like script.

Eric pushed open the door and light filled a room, about 25 feet by 60 feet. "When you walk in, you smell the odor of a century's worth of grit, grind, and physical development," Harry recalled. Having worked out there many times, I can tell you that it was not a place for anyone with a weak stomach.

They were met with Hank Williams' song, "A Country Boy Can Survive", cranked up so loud that it nearly drowned out the metallic thud of heavy weights dropping. At the very end of the room, by the squat racks, eight guys were lifting weights. Harry noticed a metal trash can on each end of the squat racks and asked Eric what they were for.

"To throw up in," he replied.

The two cadets did some bench presses. Eric had told Harry about the team's captain. Harry was stunned to realize that the description he thought was an exaggeration didn't do justice to the man.

"He was like a Nordic god! He could have been a superhero in a movie," Harry said. And let me add that Harry himself is a badass you don't mess with. "The guy was six-foot-two, red hair, light skin, tight crew cut. He had massive shoulders and a 31-inch waist. He had to have his cadet trousers custom-made because his quads were so big, but the rest of his body was so lean."

Harry watched this powerful lifter. The guy had his knees wrapped and wore a large lifting belt. He was wearing sweatpants and a t-shirt. He stood up and positioned himself under the bar, ready to lift. Just before he grabbed the bar, the cadet took off his sweatpants. Harry was shocked to see that this massive muscle man was wearing a hot pink thong under his pants!

With his back to Harry, the lifter popped up the weight and dropped it back on the rack. Suddenly, the big man whirled around to face Harry, pointing his finger at him.

He barked, "You know why I wear this? When I wear this, it makes me feel sexy, and when I feel sexy, I feel strong, and that's all that matters."

And certainly there wasn't a person in that room who would dare question his choice.

"Whatever helps a soldier to fight better is good—barring drugs or compromising your integrity," Harry explained.

The Animal House was filled with cadets finding their motivation. It might be a pink thong. Find what works for you and own it.

So, what pumps up your energy, excitement, and desire to perform at your maximum? If you don't have that passion, try to explore and understand why you're lacking it. Find your "Why" (Chapter 7), the critical source of motivation that pushes you beyond the moments when you're tempted to give in. Study what passionate people have in common (Chapter 11) so you can nurture that positive energy in yourself.

> **A cadet will not lie, cheat, or steal, or tolerate those who do.**
>
> —West Point Honor Code

THE LETTER THAT GOT ME IN TROUBLE

Remember when I said earlier in this chapter that I had made one really stupid choice as a cadet at West Point? In the interest of total candor, I'm going to share a hard lesson I learned. I'm not proud of it, but it was as valuable and lasting as anything else I gained during my four years there.

I was a junior, which makes you a "Cow" in cadet terms. It refers to "the cows coming home", meaning cadets choosing to return. Sophomores or second-years are known as "Yearlings", because they've completed one year. Seniors are "Firsties", a reference to having only one year left to go.

So, as a Cow, I had earned a weekend away. I decided to take Chris (then, my girlfriend; later, my wife) to a nearby ski resort for the weekend. The hotel experience wasn't what I expected. They elevated the price for the weekend package I had booked and then gave us a lousy room. I spoke to the person in charge at the time, who did nothing. I guess he didn't feel compelled to cater to a couple of "kids".

I was pissed. After that weekend, I wrote a letter to the manager, expressing my dissatisfaction with the quality of the visit and the lack of concern for our comfort. Then, I referenced my standing as a West Point Cadet, somehow thinking that I deserved more respect from this business because of my status at the Academy.

Instead of responding to me, the resort manager forwarded my letter to his congressman. He, in turn, sent my letter to the Commandant at West Point.

I was called into the Commandant's office, unaware of the reason, but nervous as hell. He presented me with my letter to the resort manager. The Commandant then advised me that a West Point Cadet does not use his position for influence. And when I say "advised", I mean that I left that office like a hound dog with my tail between my legs. I was embarrassed and humbled, while also accepting the responsibility to think bigger and beyond myself to represent an organization. Life is not measured by credentials. It's about who you may affect by your actions that should determine your choices.

My punishment for this transgression was what they called, "walking tours". Basically, during any unscheduled time, I had to march back and forth in the freezing cold, with a rifle on my shoulder for HOURS at a time. I can honestly say it was one of the worst experiences of my entire military life. One hundred hours of walking tours was a solid reminder that I would never think about my organization, culture, or brand in harm's way again, over something so personal. Ever.

> *"Life is not measured by credentials.*
>
> *Who you may affect by your actions should determine your choices. "*

What exactly was the lesson? Whether I thought I deserved better or not, I should have based my actions on the experience, not who or what I thought I deserved. I should have recognized that, as a customer, I was entitled to better treatment from the resort's staff. When I assumed that being a West Point Cadet put me above their other customers, I acted contrary to the honor of my position and the institution I represented.

Your rank, title, or position has no merit. You don't deserve more because you believe your title has earned those rewards. I hold my team members accountable, along with myself, for the good of everyone, not because I'm a CEO brandishing power. That would be bullying, not leadership.

THE 2020 WEST POINT CHEATING SCANDAL

In the goal to build leaders, integrity is an integral part of the West Point experience. The honor code says, "A cadet will not lie, cheat, or steal, or tolerate those who do."

In early 2020, West Point closed its campus due to the COVID-19 pandemic. In May of that year, 73 cadets allegedly cheated on a calculus test. All but one of the accused cheaters were plebes. The Academy's leadership reviewed the situation, which represented the largest cheating scandal in the school's history. Each case went before the cadet honor committee, a board of their peers. As a cadet, I led that committee, and without a doubt, cheating would have been grounds for expelling the cadet.

Lt. General Darryl A. Williams, Superintendent of the U.S. Military Academy at West Point, issued a statement that allowed for an unexpected level of leniency.

"The global pandemic disrupted our developmental process. In an instant, our tried and tested leadership model was interrupted and for a short time the Corps was dispersed to 4,400 locations around the world. In this environment, our Cadets were void of those critical developmental engagements in the barracks, in the classrooms, and on the athletic fields that help them understand themselves and increase their commitment to the West Point and Army values."

The school's leadership took responsibility for the poor choices of their cheating cadets. They interpreted that the actions were not a fair reflection of character. Instead, the indiscretion resulted from cadets being physically distanced from the leadership model before they had gained essential values.

The cadets involved were given options. Those who held themselves accountable for their actions would be enrolled in the Special Leader Development Program for Honor, "a rigorous program of personal reflection and growth that is roughly equivalent to a 2.0 credit course." The program includes about 50 hours with a developmental coach.

Ultimately, only eight cadets were expelled. Four cadets were acquitted, and two cases were dropped due to lack of evidence. Six cadets resigned. The remainder were held back for six months or a year, lost their rank and privileges, and given suspended separation, which means any violation of their probation would be cause for expulsion. 52 of the guilty cadets had been athletes but were kicked off the teams as they were deemed unworthy of representing West Point.

What happened to the Honor Code?

> **As a plebe, you might not understand how to field strip an M16, but you do know when you're cheating on a test.**
>
> —Jim Young

Going into West Point, you know it's going beyond a brutal test of your strength—physical AND mental. That's purposeful because there is no room for weakness when tough decisions need to be made. As a cadet, you have signed up for something unique. Your parents aren't there to step in and rescue you. You are on your own to rise up and meet the challenges that this training delivers, motivated by the desire to become the person you want to be.

The decision to give the Cadets a second chance was unique. In the past, we didn't see this level of tolerance when it came to violating the Honor Code.

Several alums voiced their personal opinions about the leniency.

"As a plebe, you might not understand how to field strip an M16 rifle, but you do know when you're cheating on a test," said Jim Young.

Accountability is a powerful character trait. It speaks to one's integrity and honesty. And it's a core value that I hold dear. Accusations and blame are counterproductive to effective, efficient problem-solving. Sometimes, when you treat the symptoms, you mask the cause. And isn't the cause where you need to focus your attention?

My path to West Point was paved with a combination of clarity, perseverance, and luck—in that order.

LIFE EQUATION LESSON

Every choice you make leads to a consequence. Weigh that outcome against your Life Equation. Does it add up? What values are you focused on to get where you want to be? Before you press on, stop and think about your answer.

FACTOR IN YOUR ANSWERS

1. *How did you decide on your career path? What other choices did you consider? Ultimately, what influenced your decision?*

2. *Have you ever stubbornly pursued a goal just to achieve it? Did you accomplish what you set out to do and was the reward what you expected?*

3. *Did you ever take a leap of faith? What was the experience and how did you feel about the result? Looking back, would you make the same choice again?*

+ CHAPTER 7

THE STRATEGY FACTOR

$$m\ (T) = f\ (P^2 + t + \mathsf{S} + a)$$

What is strategy? It's a plan of action to achieve a desired result. You include strategy every day of your life. You prioritize what you need to get done in a day. You organize a get-together with your friends, which requires that you take into consideration what you want to happen—like who should attend, where and when it will take place, and how you will communicate with everyone.

You apply strategy to plenty of smaller things, but do you look at the bigger picture of your life goals? Have you taken the time to prioritize all the people, actions, and choices that will make a difference for you? When you think about the decision-making process—the way you make your choices that directly impact your future—strategy must be the foundation.

Strategy is your roadmap, marking the way from where you are now to where you want to be. Imagine finding your way without GPS. [Yes, some of us remember what it was like to navigate without a little voice telling us every turn to take.] Would you head out on a trip without knowing your destination? When you live your life without a strategy, that's exactly what you're doing.

For me, a military education and an entrepreneurial career instilled the importance of strategy. I'm truly thankful for that. It has been an essential factor in my Life Equation, and I hope you'll consider strategy to be included in yours in some way.

> *"Would you head out on a trip without knowing your destination?*
>
> *When you live your life without a strategy, that's what you're doing."*

WHERE ARE YOU GOING?

Just about every job interview I ever had included the question, "Where do you see yourself in five years?" Now that I'm on the other side, conducting the interview, I know that the only value of this question is to determine if the applicant actually <u>has</u> an action plan.

The more insightful interviewer will say, "Tell me about your life plan." Then, they evaluate the candidate based on the vision they communicate for their own future. If it's vague, the person is not someone who has a clear goal. They are taking life as it comes. They haven't looked at how opportunities contribute to moving closer to a goal. A motivated, self-directed individual makes for a great team member.

> *"Sometimes you need a kick in the butt to remind you where you're going...and why."*

By this point, you know that my goal since I was in high school had been to go to West Point and then to serve my country. I was smacked with obstacles along the way—like that dang tree. When I hit a crossroad of a tough decision, I was lucky to have a father who reminded me of my goal. When considering whether to resign my commission after Marion Military Institute, Dad put me back on course with a simple reminder of my destination. My goal wasn't just an officer's commission. My primary target was West Point. After fully exploring what the U.S. Military Academy had to offer, I committed to getting there, the next milestone in fulfilling the goal of becoming a great leader. Sometimes, you need a kick in the butt to remind you where you're going…and why.

If you have that target, write it down. Stick it on your refrigerator, laptop, night table, and your car's dashboard. Keep a steady reminder of your chosen destination and you are far less likely to veer off course.

> *"Keep a steady reminder of your destination and you are far less likely to veer off course."*

KNOW YOUR "WHY"

Where do you even start with formulating a strategy? Determine where you want to go and why you want to achieve that goal. Strategy answers your "How?", but you need to understand and buy into "Why". No strategy in the world will guide you to success if you're not one hundred percent motivated to get there. Every little doubt is like a crack in your foundation. Eventually, your motivation falls through and you abandon goals that could have changed your life.

How many times have you started a new year with a resolution? You're going to lose weight, stop smoking, give up chocolate, or be nicer to your in-laws. The problem here is your "Why". What's your motivation for making this change? If it's simply the date on the calendar, don't waste your time. Before February rolls around, something has drilled cracks in your resolution because it wasn't supported by a powerful "Why".

*"Every little doubt is a crack
in your foundation.*

*Eventually, your motivation
falls through and you abandon goals
that could have changed your life."*

You've probably heard people talk about "living with purpose". It might sound cliché, and for some, it is. But you're reading this book, which tells me you're committed to finding your own Life Equation.

In his bestselling book, *"Find Your Why: A Practical Guide for Discovering Purpose For You and Your Team"*[1], author Simon Sinek writes, "Happiness comes from what we do. Fulfillment comes from why we do it."

WHEN TWO BRAINS COLLIDE

My colleague, David Camp, is a master of strategy. When I was looking to fill the position of Vice President of Sales at Legacy International, I knew I needed someone who could find the right balance between logic and creativity. David is one of those rare people who lives somewhere between his left brain (linear) and right brain (creative), depending on the mission. Shortly after David joined our team, I saw the immense value of his perspective on developing strategy. Although I'm not big on titles, we agreed to expand David's role to Senior Vice President of Strategy and Innovation. Like all of our job titles, they exist on business cards and org charts. A strong team doesn't need labels. They know exactly what their roles are.

David likes to tell a story that shows how he and I complement one another. Many years ago, he and I were walking down a sidewalk in a community where we had been contracted to handle sales and marketing. We came to a corner. I followed the sidewalk while David took a shortcut across a lawn. He asked me why I stayed on

---

1 Sinek, Simon, David Mead, and Peter Docker, "Find Your Why: Discovering Purpose For You and Your Team", 2017

"A strong team doesn't need labels. They know exactly what their roles are. "

the sidewalk when I could have also cut across the lawn and saved a few steps. It never occurred to me to stray off the paved path.

> *"He asked me why I stayed on the sidewalk.*
> *It never occurred to me to stray off the*
> *paved path."*

It was probably my military training. There was a sidewalk that was intended for people to walk on, so I was respecting that purpose. In my mind, you don't veer from the chartered course. His nature told him to take a shorter route from Point A to Point B. We were heading to the same destination but chose different paths. He followed his creative right brain and I was driven by my linear left brain. Of course, choosing whether to walk on the sidewalk isn't a life-changing decision but it does accurately reflect the difference in our ways of thinking. And because we have different but complementary perspectives on strategy, we've been able to see much farther, examine more scenarios, and avoid more pitfalls than if we were to work separately.

Remember that your strategy needs to make sense to you. It doesn't matter how other people map out their action plan. Do what fits your character, style, ability, and goals.

THE CAMP APPROACH TO STRATEGY

When David Camp came on board at Legacy International, he immediately studied our goals and processes to weigh each component against its contribution to hitting our targets. He unraveled each of them, astutely measuring every facet against its contribution to the ultimate goal. Does this step take us closer or simply delay the process? David looks at strategy like this:

"Strategy is mapping out the most successful, predictable result. It guides you from Point A to Point B, achieving results every step of the way."

When David joined Legacy International, we were working with a developer of resort property in The Bahamas. Legacy International was hired for our marketing and sales services. We were going to start with pre-sales because the development hadn't yet developed. We were selling the experience, without any tangible homes to present yet.

I had my doubts about the project right from the start but decided to take on the challenge. There was a lot to do, and we were starting without quite a few key items. The developer had promised to do the preparation and be ready for us, every step of the way. Unfortunately, he didn't come through and we were scrambling to make up for what we didn't have. How can you deliver the promised results when you don't have what was promised? Well, we tried.

David dissected the project's goal (pre-sales of resort homes), opportunities (great location, gorgeous homes, resort amenities), and challenges. Ok, I'm not going parenthetical here on the challenges because there were just too many to squeeze into one sentence. The developer had a big vision for this property. In fact, I think his vision was so broad that he couldn't see the sequence of many small steps that would take him there.

But David and I did.

We built a strategy based on Legacy's proprietary five-stage process. We included all the ingredients needed to achieve the aggressive pre-sales goal. Our client was excited. He was relieved to have the help he had been missing to push this resort property along.

The developer had his own goal: Sell out the waterfront condominiums. His "strategy" was to engage professionals to get it done. Period. You can't just hire a sales organization and consider it done. You need refinement of the real estate project and product definition, in addition to sales systems and processes. Just thinking that engaging a sales organization alone and thinking you're done is like deciding that your strategy for achieving financial success is to win the lottery. When you want something enough, you fully invest in making it happen.

We attempted to move forward on marketing this resort property, but it was like trying to drive a car with only three wheels. Progress was slow because we weren't adequately equipped to move efficiently and successfully to the destination. We utilized our sales strategy, which had proven successful with other developers, but without the cooperation of an integral stakeholder, it was a lost cause.

> *"To appreciate a good strategy,*
> *you must recognize a bad one."*

Ultimately, we agreed that it just wasn't in our best interest to put our resources behind a project that the developer himself didn't support.

Why do I share a story of failure with you? Because to appreciate a good strategy, you must recognize a bad one—or the total lack of one.

ART + SCIENCE = STRATEGY

A solid strategy for achieving any goal is based on two factors:

1. **Art:** The interpretive part of your strategy, one that is based on psychology and emotional response

2. **Science:** The physical, tangible actions and responses that influence an outcome

These are polar opposites. But, like yin and yang, they are reliable opposites that fit and function seamlessly together when used in the right proportions.

The Art side of strategy planning reflects emotional responses. The person who excels at this is the storyteller—like the salesperson who tells you what it's like to drive that car and manages to ignite your excitement.

The Science-driven person likes processes. There's a proven method to follow, step by step. In sales, for example, this person might explain one feature, sell you on it, and then move to the next. But they only take you to the next selling point when you have fully embraced the current one.

To put this in perspective, look at the set of a movie. The actor has a script. That's the tangible (Science) component. Then, the actor interprets the script and adds emotion and movement. That's the intangible (Art) side. The artful person excels in interpreting the words. The scientific one follows the script without ad libbing. Or the artful one cuts across a yard while the scientific counterpart follows the paved path.

Ideally, you blend both Art and Science into your strategy.

ART + SCIENCE = INTERVIEW SUCCESS

Your goal is to land your dream job. You have the interview, but what is your plan of action for getting the job offer?

SCIENCE: The physical aspects

1. Research the company to ask intelligent questions during the interview.

2. Present yourself in professional attire and demeanor.

3. Speak clearly.

4. Arrive five minutes early for your scheduled interview, whether it's a video call or in person.

5. ART: The interpretive components

6. Pay attention to the interviewer's spoken and unspoken communication (body language); the interviewer interprets your focus as good listening skills.

7. When the interviewer asks, "Where do you see yourself in five years?" respond with a succinct overview of your career plan, demonstrating your passion to learn and grow and how this job and this company fit into this vision.

Or…you could go into the interview without a strategy. You've dressed appropriately, but you failed to map out an action plan for the interview's conversation.

"You don't often get a second chance, so prepare yourself to take on challenges as they come."

If you're the interviewer, which candidate would be more appealing to you?

WHICH SIDE ARE YOU ON?

Some people rely more heavily on one side of the strategy equation. They might be the empathic ones who look at how their choices impact other people. Conversely, someone who is more method-driven examines the physical steps of the strategy.

If you want to see where you fall in the art-science strategic continuum, try this. Your goal is to plan a vacation.

1. Make a list of how you will plan your vacation.

2. Next, on a piece of paper, draw a vertical line down the middle of the paper.

3. Mark the left side of the paper as "Art" and the right side as "Science".

4. Take each item from #1 and assign it to one side, Art or Science.

The "Art" or magic consists of the part of the trip that is unnecessary or inessential. These components are the things that stir imagination and create memories. For example, playing "I Spy" on a long road trip or making sure the area around the hotel has options for some spontaneous fun would be Art. It could be the photo booth where you create memories and the lei being placed around your neck when you first step foot on the island. Art is the novelty of the trip. It opens the window to the unexpected. It's the chocolate mint left on the pillow.

The "Science" or logic of the trip is reflected in the essential aspects: when you leave, when you return, where you stay, etc. These are clearly defined and quantitative.

As you build your list to see where you fall on the Art-Science scale, notice where the weight is heavier. Does one side have more items than the other? If so, you should work on incorporating more items that reflect the opposite side of the strategy equation of Art + Science = Strategy.

STRATEGY MATTERS

Obviously, you need strategy in your career or business. Skipping over strategy is like building a house without a blueprint. There isn't anything to guide you in the most effective, efficient direction to achieve the desired results. And you could end up having the roof cave in on you.

> *"Skipping over strategy is like building a house without a blueprint."*

For the same reason, you should incorporate strategy in your Life Equation. You want to go to a good college? How are you going to achieve that? You want to get into a highly competitive field? Are you going to trust "dumb luck"?

I learned from a young age that having a goal wasn't good enough. With all the obstacles that landed in my path to West Point, I could have easily given up and chosen another destination. But I don't like giving up. You shouldn't either.

> *"Giving up is giving in. You're the one missing out."*

Giving up is giving in, and at the end of the day, you're the one missing out. I guarantee you that West Point would not have suffered from not having me as a cadet there. The Army Special Ops certainly could have recruited and trained another helicopter pilot in my place. And any job I've had in my life could have been filled by someone else.

But I didn't give up or give in. And it's all because I had a strategy to follow. Get into West Point by working hard—for my grades, on the football field, and in the commitments I made. I didn't plan for the car accident, but I did a work-around. The doctor predicted a long-term recovery for me. I chose to be more aggressive and fight back harder to shorten that return to peak shape.

When I finally entered West Point, two years older than my fellow plebes (first-years), I had a strategy to utilize what I had learned at Marion Military Institute to be the best cadet I could be. My strategy was the same as I had used in high school. Work hard and rely on integrity for decision-making.

I admit that West Point made my high school years look like a summer vacation. I wasn't prepared for the rigors and intensity that hit you smack in the face every single day. But on those occasions when I felt my resolve weakening, I dug down into the depths of my conviction to follow my strategy, "Never give up." When I was a member of the 160th Special Operations Aviation Regiment, a group of elite soldiers known as "Night Stalkers", this relentlessness was a plus for me. In a group whose motto is "Night Stalkers Don't Quit", I already had the mindset firmly ingrained in me.

THE 7-STEP APPROACH TO DECISION-MAKING

The military teaches a process for making a decision. It's called the "Military Decision Making Process" and, like all things military, it's known by its acronym: MDMP.

MDMP is a complex set of seven steps to follow, with each one based on careful analysis of opportunities and possible outcomes. The process "helps leaders apply thoroughness, clarity, sound judgment, logic, and professional knowledge to understand situations, develop options to solve problems, and reach decisions."[2]

Here are the MDMP's seven steps:

1. **Receipt of Mission:** The commander receives and reviews the orders to determine the needs.

2. **Mission Analysis:** Examine the mission and problem statement, commander's intent, and criteria for course of action.

---

2 Wade, Norman, M, (2015) "BSS5: The Battle Staff SMARTbook, 5th Ed. (Leading, Planning & Conducting Military Operations)"; Lightning Press. https://www.thelightningpress.com/smart-books/bss5-battle-staff/

3. **Course of Action (COA) Development:** Create course of action statements that incorporate updated planning guidance.

4. **COA Analysis:** The "war game" that presents potential decision points and initial assessment measures.

5. **COA Comparison:** Using the information gathered to this point, evaluate the COA and recommend a COA with updated assessments.

6. **COA Approval:** Get approval and make necessary adjustments.

7. **Orders Production, Dissemination, and Transition:** Submit the order and ensure subordinates understand the plan.

When you're making choices that affect lives, it's understandable that the leaders want to be absolutely certain you're following a proven methodology. MDMP guides decision-makers to make the best choice through careful analysis that looks at all conceivable contingencies. You're basically sifting through the action plan at a micro level. As you can imagine, it's very thorough.

Military strategists use their knowledge and experience to project outcomes. *"If I do this, then experience shows that this will happen. Is that the result I want? Does it lead me on the right path to the ultimate conclusion I'm aiming for?"* Everything is considered before a decision is made. They derive multiple courses of action, associated with the challenges that might happen along the way.

These military leaders leave absolutely nothing to chance. Lives are on the line—the lives of the soldiers who are executing the orders and the civilians who are affected by the outcome. You reduce risk and maximize success with this exhaustive level of detailed strategic planning. Sure, your choices might not be life-and-death but they're important to your success. Treat them with the same level of consideration.

I had told you earlier that my father was also a great decision-maker. Like the military and its MDMP, he had a process. He told me, "Stop. Take a breath. Study all the outcomes. Put your faith in God. Choose the answer that best represents you and you will be fine. And keep a positive attitude."

However you reach your decisions, apply a strategy. You'll have a consistent path to follow, one that has proven to serve you time and time again. But if that strategy hasn't worked, start over. Just don't give up.

NO GROUNDHOG DAYS

You're going to live each day once, so you might as well plan your strategy. You rarely get a second chance, so prepare yourself to take on challenges as they come. In the movie, "Groundhog Day", Bill Murray was a cynical television weatherman who was forced to keep reliving one day until he righted the many mistakes he made on that day. In the real world, there is no "Groundhog Day" scenario in which you go back and relive your past until you get it right. No "do-overs". You can't change what has happened, but you CAN control what WILL happen by developing and executing a life strategy.

> *"You don't often get a second chance,*
> *so prepare yourself to*
> *take on challenges as they come."*

THE DECISION TREE

If you're not inclined to delve into the intricate MDMP process, a decision tree is an excellent alternative. A decision tree, also known as information mapping, is like making a list of pros and cons, but the process pushes you to dig deeper into the various aspects of your options.

With a decision tree, you start with the trunk. This reflects the choice you have to make. Add a branch for each decision that contributes to the ultimate one. Then branch out from each limb with every possible outcome. Keep going until your tree sprouts fully in every way you can imagine. Once you've fully created the decision tree, you can see where you want to go. Then use this visual to map out your action plan.

Here's an example. My goal was to attend West Point and graduate with an officer's commission. I learned that I had a two-year wait to be accepted there because of my medical disqualification. At that time, I had four options:

1. Enroll in another college or university.

2. Do something that doesn't involve higher education.

3. Get a job, wait out the two years, and re-apply to West Point.

4. Enroll in a military junior academy.

#1 and #2 were never options for me. The conventional route or a decision of no higher education just didn't appeal to me

If I chose #3, I could eventually achieve my goal. But there were a few limbs to look at. Was I willing to (a) wait two years, bearing in mind I was a headstrong, anxious 18-year-old guy and a Texan; and (b) take the risk that I might not be accepted in two years?

What would #4 do for me? It would put me on the right path toward going to West Point and earning an officer's commission. HOWEVER, while I would graduate from the military junior academy with an officer's commission, I could not keep it if I enrolled at West Point. In addition, I would enter West Point as a first-year plebe, because the credit for my two years of studies would not transfer. So, with the fourth option, I had to consider whether I was willing to invest two years of my education and then give up the officer's commission to attend West Point.

I chose to resign my commission and start all over at West Point. What would YOU have done in this situation?

LIFE EQUATION LESSON

If you're still with me here, we're on a good path to building a Life Equation that works for you. No matter what you decide to incorporate in yours, consider the importance of Strategy being a factor. When you leave choices up to chance, you give up control of the one thing in this world over which you should have total command— your life path.

FACTOR IN YOUR ANSWERS

1. *Have you consciously applied strategy to your life? What was the plan of attack and how did it contribute to the outcome?*

2. *Do you make New Year's resolutions? What is the longest you've maintained a resolution and what was it? Did you share your commitment with others?*

3. *Are there areas in your life that would benefit from establishing and following a strategy? How could you incorporate the "Art and Science" of strategy to achieve results?*

+ CHAPTER 8

LESSONS LEARNED AND EARNED FROM SPECIAL OPS

Are you prepared to take on challenges head on? Do you thrive on pushing yourself to do more? It's been said that life begins outside your comfort zone. Even one small step can take you to a higher level. But how far are you willing to go to overcome a challenge?

You've probably seen some of the movies about Special Operations, like *"Blackhawk Down"* and *"Lone Survivor"*. Maybe you've met someone who served as a Navy SEAL (Sea, Air and Land), Green Beret, Delta, Ranger, or Special Operator—and I mean the ones who actually served, not the many pretenders. Don't get me started.

> *"To prepare for what could happen, Special Operators undergo intense experiences that only a small minority of people could endure."*

You may already have your perception of these elite military forces. I encourage you to get past the machismo you've seen portrayed. The men and women who are chosen for Special Ops challenges are smart, dedicated, and brave individuals who put their lives on the line in service to their country. They engage in missions that require far more strategic and tactical preparation than the regular military. To prepare for what could happen, Special Operators undergo intense experiences that only a small minority of people could endure. Yes, they're tough and confident. They need to be in order to perform their duties with the precision that's required. But you won't find a loud braggart among any group of Special Operators. The honor that comes with being a Special Operator is revered by those who were chosen. They don't entertain people with stories of their missions. Your position is not your credentials; your character is.

I was honored to serve with the 160th Special Operations Aviation Regiment (SOAR), which provides helicopter support to all military Special Operations. Also known as "Night Stalkers", our covert missions were usually executed at night. As a Quick Response Force (QRF), we were prepared to handle an extensive variety of aerial missions. We trained to operate helicopters in tough environments (water, desert, and extreme weather) where we had to manage the impact of the rotor blades on a challenging landing surface. We even practiced landing on carrier decks and submarines and in urban settings like rooftops. We also became proficient at aerial refueling, an essential skill to keep mission-critical aircraft in the air.

There are some truly valuable lessons to be learned from the people who trained and served in the United States Special Operations. Every day of my life since I left Special Ops, I have used the knowledge and experience I gained during my service, both in my personal and professional lives. And I've passed them along to friends, family, and colleagues who have then put that knowledge into practice. So, as you consider your own Life Equation, think about what you can gain from the hard lessons from members of Special Operations Forces.

"Every time you decide you're incapable of achieving a task or goal, you make it a certainty."

YOUR ONLY LIMIT IS YOU

There is no "I can't" in the military. Saying "I can't" translates to "I won't". And that attitude would never fly in Special Ops. Closing your mind is limiting your opportunities. Every time you decide you're incapable of achieving a task or goal, you make it a certainty.

Your attitude is the only barrier to achievement. You'd be amazed at what you can accomplish when you are fully dedicated to what you want and with the right mindset.

Setting a goal to get into Special Ops came from a lifelong habit of setting the bar high for myself. I wanted West Point because it was something bigger, and happened to provide the best leadership training available. From there, I chose aviation because it was the most specialized and challenging career path. I often asked myself, "What would it take to be the best?"

Some might call this attitude "achievement junkie". I won't disagree, but I have never taken on a challenge just to experience the thrill. The "Why" was much bigger. The decision has always been to become a better version of myself and to make a positive impact on the world.

I was stationed at Fort Campbell, Kentucky—home of the 101st Airborne Air Assault Division, known as the "Screaming Eagles"—flying the Chinook helicopter every day, in training and missions. Across the tarmac was the 160th SOAR regimental headquarters. I became curious and discovered it was a covert aviation unit, known to include the best pilots in the business. During my years of service flying helicopters with the regular Army, I had aimed for Pilot in Command status. It's a notable achievement, usually reserved for warrant officer pilots. To get to Pilot in Command, you had to complete a lot of flight time and lead missions. It is not common for a commissioned officer to achieve this level because they were splitting time between flying and leading teams, so they didn't accumulate enough flying time.

But...I got there. I earned Pilot in Command in spite of the naysayers. Not satisfied, I wanted to keep going upward in my career (no pun intended). It was an easy choice to set my sights on this next level: SOAR.

There's a saying among the SOAR community: "You don't choose the 160th; the 160th chooses you." You don't seek them out. Whether I wanted it or not, they had to find me. The first thing that will disqualify you is your attitude. The motorcycle-riding Tom Cruise type would never get past the first step of the screening. That kind of individual is not trainable. Without that ability, you're not a team type of person and that makes you unreliable. In life-and-death situations, Special Operators need to follow the process precisely. There's no room for a Maverick.

"The motorcycle-riding, Tom Cruise type would never get past the first step of the screening. That kind of individual is not trainable."

My fellow SOAR pilot, Kirk Keepers, told me about an aviator he served with. Like Kirk, He and Matt were both Captains and Instructor Pilots who were interested in joining the 160th. The process starts with an invitation, either because you submitted an application or they scouted you out, whether you were aware of it or not.

Kirk and Matt applied. Matt received his invitation for Special Ops assessment before Kirk.

"When I go up there and I get in, I will put in a good word for you. It's a lot about knowing people," Matt told Kirk.

Matt would never fulfill that promise because he didn't pass the evaluation. He said Matt certainly strutted with the Top Gun veneer and the SOAR evaluators probably recognized it immediately. Kirk went shortly after and was accepted.

Before going for his own assessment, Kirk received valuable advice from a friend. "Don't be a jerk."

"Special Ops looks for people who aren't arrogant," Kirk explained. "You're going to be working with them in small groups and for potentially a long time. You should be self-confident, but not cocky. We had a saying, that there are people *IN* the 160th and people who *ARE* the 160th. It doesn't matter if you've been there ten days or ten years. Some will change, thinking they're hot shit because they're in, but that's not who and what the unit is."

A TOUGH START

The initial evaluation for Special Ops includes financial and background checks, because even the tiniest flaw could create a situation that causes a Special Operator additional hardship—and that compromises your performance. You also undergo a huge array of psychological tests to determine if you have the personality traits and behaviors that enable you to perform at the highest level.

Once you get through the initial selection process for Special Ops, you go in and you go fast. There's a six-month training program to see if you meet the requirements of an operator. The highly proficient, extensive training covers land navigation, weapons, and overall survival/combative techniques.

The breaking point, if you haven't already fallen out, is SERE School—Survival Evasion Resistance and Escape. This part of your training is designed to teach you how to avoid capture and, if captured, prepare you to endure captivity. Special Ops trainees undergo the Level C program, designed for soldiers whose assignments put them at a high risk of being captured. Level C training is done at only a few military bases in the country.

"We exist to teach soldiers and individuals what to do when the situation goes from bad to far worse," explained SERE Instructor Harry Haug. [1]

Given the nature of the missions, learning intense survival techniques and proving the ability to handle the pressure are absolutely essential. If one soldier fails, he puts his entire team at risk.

When you begin, you have no idea how long it will last. You start by trying to avoid capture, using your training to survive while also evading the enemy. Inevitably, because it's part of the program, you ARE captured. You're taken to a prison—a place that, I assure

---

[1] SERE Survival and Resistance School, https://usmilitary.com/sere-survival-and-resistance-school/.

you, is a realistic simulation of a POW camp. Deafening music is played to rattle you. You're deprived of sleep in an attempt to break you down. And the physical conditions are unlike anything you've experienced in your life.

There's a lot more detail to the program and the experience that I will not detail here in order to protect the integrity of the SERE School. I just want to include the information that is public so you can understand what happens in this rigorous program.

"You're taken to a prison— a place that is a realistic simulation of a POW camp."

For an indefinite amount of time, we were pushed to the limits. Isolation, hunger, and sleep deprivation; and application of psychological techniques continued throughout the days and nights. The challenge during this facet of SERE School was to figure out an escape tactic.

Every soldier had the choice to bow out at any time. They would simply ring the bell and leave. The sounds of the bell became more frequent as the time passed. I don't know how long each soldier lasted before ringing the bell, because we had no concept of time in that dark place. I do remember steeling my resolve with each clang of that damn bell.

There are specific safety regulations for this training, but you are not going to emerge unscathed. Unbeknownst to me before beginning this experience, I was the Senior Ranking Officer (SRO), which meant I was responsible for my team—leading, protecting, and taking the punishment for them. You were expected to tell your "captors" nothing. Once they figured out who the SRO was—and they did—you're targeted. When a member of your team made a mistake, the SRO took the punishment. That's plenty of motivation to pull your team together and lead them.

As "prisoners", we were taken out for fifteen-minute intervals, during which we carefully observed our surroundings and tools. We worked as a team, sharing our observations and using our training to develop an escape plan. Throughout our captivity, I thought only about escape. Although truly exhausted, my senses were still sharp. During those brief periods outside, I looked around to weigh my opportunities and to communicate with my team. Every single moment of limited freedom was an exercise in strategic thinking and laser-focused decision-making.

On one of these "breaks", we stood at attention, facing the enemy. We were told to turn around and face the other way. My heart was beating and my mind was racing through scenarios of what was about to happen.

Then, I saw the trainers standing in a line in front of us. It took a few moments before I understood that we had completed the test—well, some of us. Many of the men who went into this POW experience with us had rung the bell before this day. Did they ever know how close they were to completing this test?

> ## *"I had made my commitment to seeing it through Special Ops training. I can't do it' was not an option."*

I admit there were many moments during SERE School when I thought about giving up. I pictured my wife and desperately wanted to be comfortable at home with her. And I thought about my dad. I wanted him to be proud. He would never know what I went through, and frankly, it didn't matter. I had made my commitment to seeing it through Special Ops training. "I can't do it" was not an option.

You have the inner strength to do more than you think you can. All you need is the "I can" mindset. What is it that holds you back? Fear of failure? Fear of rejection? Limits of time, money, or other resources?

There is always a way to achieve the goals that really matter. It starts with believing in yourself.

*"There is always a way to achieve
the goals that really matter.*

It starts with believing in yourself."

"NO" IS A START, NOT AN END

"No" can be a hard stop, like "I can't." When you shift your self-talk to believing you can do more, work harder, and overcome whatever stands in your way, you realize that you must look at obstacles in a different way.

In Special Ops, we were trained to seek alternate solutions, to explore contingencies for bypassing an impasse.

Kirk Keepers told me his desire to get into Special Ops was because "people said I couldn't." He wanted to be with "the tip of the spear types" but knew he had a few hoops to jump through.

Kirk was serving in Army Aviation at Fort Campbell, Kentucky, when he first inquired about getting into the 160th SOAR Regiment. Having undergone two major shoulder surgeries during his service, Kirk was told, "Oh, wait a few years. You're not getting the fly time. You don't have enough experience."

Being the badass he is, he kept pushing until he did have the experience.

*"Kirk is one of those people who never
backs down from a challenge, never uses
limitations as an excuse to give up, and
can be counted on to come through.*

*That's what made him a successful Special
Operator and a Special Human."*

The Army invited Kirk to join the nuclear program, to become a nuclear inspector. He had a science degree, but would need an advanced degree, which the government would support.

As he was pondering the option, Kirk told his dad, "I could do this and it's a great job. Or I can get assessed for the 160th."

His father responded exactly as my own dad would have. "You can always go to school."

Kirk is one of those people who loves to prove people wrong when they underestimate his resolve. He never backs down from a challenge, doesn't use limitations as an excuse to give up, and can be counted on to come through. That's what made him a successful Special Operator and Special Human.

There will always be people who tell you "No". You can accept it at face value or dig in to get to "Yes".

YOUR TRAINING IS NEVER COMPLETE

When young adults come out of high school, they experience a feeling of accomplishment and rightfully so. In their young lives, that's a major milestone. But beyond graduation day, that feeling fades as the next level of learning hits them square in the face. They go onto college or training for a career.

Whether you climb the corporate ladder or earn advanced degrees, you're never done training. Every day presents another opportunity to learn. The lesson might happen because you're paying attention to what's happening around you or your knowledge could be the result of dedicated, purposeful training. Regardless of the source, accept that you can never know enough, can never be great enough.

"Accept that you can never know enough, can never be great enough."

When I completed Special Ops training, I was a proficient soldier—proficient at flying a Chinook in dangerous situations that might lead to my capture and even death. Every day of my service, we trained. The goal was to complete an exercise within plus-or-minus 30 seconds of the target time. The purpose of such exhaustive preparation is to remove all room for error. When you work as a team, you rely on each person to perform their duties to their best potential. In Special Ops, you count on those team members to execute their portion of the mission with precision. There's no room for doubts that someone will be in position when and where you need them to be. Frequently, there is no conversation during a mission. You depend on the knowledge that each of you is highly trained and ready to go. Because if you're not, things can go wrong to the extreme of someone paying the ultimate sacrifice: giving up their life.

> *"The phrase 'killing time' should be taken seriously.*
>
> *Every opportunity you waste will only subtract from your own success.*
>
> *Someday, you'll regret killing that time."*

That's extreme, but what if you approached your own life with the same commitment to improving yourself? Instead of binge-watching a show, you could expand your knowledge. Take an online course, practice a skill, read a book. LEARN! You have one life, built from a series of moments. The phrase "killing time" should be taken seriously, because every opportunity you waste will only subtract from your own success. It's a crime in which you are both the victim and the perpetrator. You don't get that time back, and someday, you'll regret killing it.

LIVE THE TRUE MEANING OF TEAMWORK

There used to be a time when we referred to "groups", particularly when it came to the workplace. At some point, the term evolved to "teams", which better reflects the connection between the people who are grouped together. You can be part of a group without participating in any way, but as a team member, you have responsibilities. Do you know at any moment what is expected of you?

What's the purpose of a team? In Chapter 4, I explained that a team is assembled with an outcome in mind. Winning is usually

> **Communicate your expectations or they will dissolve into resentment when they're not met.**

the objective, and it's up to your team to determine exactly what defines a "win".

For a team to be victorious, it needs to function as one unit that is focused on a goal. That goal is understood and fully embraced by every member. If you look at championship teams, you see a group of players who work tirelessly together, each one playing their best, performing their unique role, and respecting their teammates. They're not watching the others to see if they're doing their job. That's unproductive and potentially damaging to the group and its results. Teams that have discord filtering through the ranks is like a chain with a missing link. One bad move by one individual can derail the outcome.

In Special Ops, we had to function seamlessly as a team. We trusted our teammates, knowing that they had undergone the same scrutiny and training to become a Special Operator. We didn't question another's competence because we each took training with the same unrelenting dedication.

In the same team spirit, we all understood that position is not the rank or the name on your uniform, but how you fit into the mission. We were equals. We shared ultimate respect for each other's competence and specialization.

One of the first things issued when I became a Special Ops team member was a pager. You might not know what a pager is, but it's how we alerted people before cell phones. When that alert went off, your response was to go, no matter where you were. You went because the team was relying on you. So many times, I would look at my wife, Chris, who had seen the pager. "I'll see you when you get back," she said every time. She didn't know where I was going or for how long. Then again, neither did I.

Chris and I were our own team. We counted on each other. She understood my role as a Special Ops team member, and I understood mine as a member of our family.

Do you live with the same commitment to your team, your family, your faith? Do you deliver on expectations? Do they? Whether you are a member or a team leader, take your role seriously. Communicate expectations or they will dissolve into resentment when they're not met. Support your teammates; don't allow petty differences or jealousies to impede your success. Use your combined strengths to be a contributing member to a championship team.

ACCOUNTABILITY STARTS AT THE TOP

As I mentioned earlier in this chapter, I was the SRO of my team of Special Ops trainees in SERE School. When we were captured and put in the simulated POW camp, that leadership meant that I was responsible for everything my team members did or didn't do. It was to my advantage to keep my team staying strong and in sync.

I didn't resent the treatment that came at me because a team member didn't respond correctly to the demands of our captors. Every instance was a training moment, for them and for me. After the damage was done, I returned to my unit and immediately put my mind to work on how to avoid the situation that led to the punishment. What did my team need to learn or to do better? When they failed, I failed.

> *"Every instance was a training moment, for them and for me.*
> *When they failed, I failed."*

That's accountability—accepting your role in a situation and owning your mistakes. Accountability is one of the key factors in my own Life Equation. I don't believe in finger-pointing. It's a useless activity and a waste of time and resources. Instead of seeking out people to blame, look at the problem. Invest in finding a better way to achieve the right result.

If you don't want your teammates to deliver excuses, be a role model for accountability. Give them the room to make mistakes. Teach them to find a way to navigate those errors, to learn from them, and move on. In this way, you also encourage them to take risks, which is the only way they will grow.

Instead of berating the group or a team member, offer them a positive direction. "You know, everyone, this didn't work out as we hoped. That simply means we have room to be better."

> *"Be a role model for accountability.*
>
> *Teach them to navigate errors, to learn and move on.*
>
> *In this way, you encourage them to take risks, which is the only way they will grow."*

Pull your team members aside for a private conversation, not a public humiliation. I remember the SERE trainers taking me aside to challenge me to look at things differently. They were trying to guide me, to learn and grow from the experience. Then I could go back and apply that insight to do better in my training.

The next time you point a finger at someone else, look at your hand. There are three other fingers pointing right back at you.

> *"The next time you point a finger at someone else, look at your hand.*
>
> *There are three other fingers pointing right back at you."*

PREPARE FOR THE 'WHAT IFs"

How many times have you started a statement with "If only I…"?

That's a sign of regret. And regret is a wasted emotion. You can't do anything to change what happened. But what you CAN do is to plan better to prevent regrettable outcomes.

Start with planning for contingencies—the "What Ifs". Special Ops taught us to commit to a critical path (a detailed roadmap to success, described in Chapter 7). This action plan demonstrated that the team leader had thought through all the possibilities that could occur during the execution of the mission. Things like weather, human error, and alternate strategies executed in the field by the target—they all had to be considered with the "if this, then that" tactical approach.

The critical path prepares the team. There is no need to re-think a situation in the field because the response has already been planned in advance. Members follow a seamless shift from one plan to the contingency. No matter where the mission takes you, you have a pre-approved strategy. Details as small as which hand you use to grab the handle on an emergency exit during a water landing comes into consideration, because it contributes to the mission's outcome.

How can you use this contingency planning outside of a mission? Imagine you're planning a special vacation. You haven't gone on a trip in years and you're making this a big one. Let's say you've decided to head out on a cross country road trip. You're going to rent a camper and start by checking online to see what's available.

You're tempted by a big camper with more features. When you go to pick it up, you discover that your vehicle can't tow the weight or you don't have the right hitch to hook it up. What do you do to overcome this obstacle?

Let's say you had visions of camping where you could have specific views. You map out a route, without learning in advance where you can find available campgrounds with the facilities you want. At some point you must decide between a shower and a cell phone signal. What would it have required of you to avoid having to make that choice?

You also brought your dog along, only to learn that the park where you planned to camp isn't pet-friendly. You go to the local kennel to board her, but don't have the required rabies certificate and vaccination records. Now what?

It's all about thinking, "What if?"

Former Special Operator Kirk Keepers says he adapted the contingency mindset in the military and lives with it to this day.

"I have the challenge of slowing my mind down from contingencies. There are a lot of 'What ifs' out there, but when you're in it, you don't think about it. You know how you're going to respond and how others will respond."

Every time he enters a building, Kirk looks for the exit. When he drives, he uses the same awareness as when he flies, remaining fully cognizant of his surroundings. "There's a semi on the right and left, and a car right behind me. I'd better accelerate out of the situation in case someone blows a tire." With this, he has a prepared response and wastes no time in adjusting to a change in the situation.

A critical path addresses the probability of an occurrence, high or low. Regardless of the odds, you prepare for the possibility. This level of preparation prevents mistakes and delays.

In my business, I have incorporated critical path planning. My team members do the same. When something isn't on track, we all know to communicate the change. The critical path is updated, and this communication keeps the project on target.

Map out your plans and you can identify the gaps as well as any additional steps that need to happen. It will definitely prevent you from getting lost in the desert without a cell phone signal.

IT'S GOOD TO LOOK BACK

Life is a series of lessons, if you're alert enough to catch them. You come out of a relationship, questioning yourself, your choices, and your actions. You might even lick your wounds by accepting the other person's statement, "It's not you, it's me."

But if you don't take the time to fully learn from the experience, you are destined to repeat it. You will continue to trust people who will disappoint. You will make choices that don't advance your progress. You might achieve success, but you won't grow.

Following every Special Ops mission, we took part in an After Action Review (AAR). This session dissected every step, every action, and every decision that contributed to the outcome of the mission. No matter how successful you thought you were, the AAR uncovered room for improvement.

For example, the person who was responsible for delivering

the ammunition to the helicopter arrived three minutes late. He couldn't explain it away with "the guy who was supposed to unlock the gate wasn't there." He needed to demonstrate accountability.

In the After Action Review, leaders asked, "Did you meet with him the day before and tell him you needed him there exactly at that time? Did you find out who his backup was? And did you talk to the backup person the day before and also let him know your time requirement?"

In an AAR, you're in a room of people who have all executed this action a thousand times before. They know what it takes and they are there to ensure that you do, too. By the end of the review, you'll have exhausted every contingency. You walk away, not feeling dejected but ready to put that learning into practice.

> *"By the end of the review, you walk away, not feeling dejected but ready to put that learning into practice."*

Wherever you are in your life, look back. Don't be satisfied with what you've done. Conduct your own After Action Review and set yourself up for continued success.

EVERY DAY IS A SPECIAL OPERATION

You don't need to be a member of Special Ops to benefit from this experience. This training puts a select few people into extreme and harsh situations that the vast majority of people will never encounter. But the insight gained can apply to anyone's life. These are fundamental lessons for living a more purposeful and predictable life that keeps you on track with your goals. A Life Equation represents a tactical approach, a guide for evaluating choices—the ones you've made, the ones you're still pondering, and those that are yet to come.

Your entire life is a special operation and you are at the helm. Be a leader with laser-focus on the goal, a strategy for handling

"If you don't fully learn from the experience, you are destined to repeat it."

the challenges, and the ability to respond with resilience, integrity, and accountability. Keep your mind open to trainable moments, for yourself and the people or the life you lead.

> *"A Life Equation represents a tactical approach for evaluating choices— the ones you've made, the ones you're still pondering, and those that are yet to come."*

What if your entire life were a Special Operation? How would you lead it?

LIFE EQUATION LESSON

Invest in preparation. Determine your goal and develop a strategy that guides your action plan. Then keep training, because your education never ends. Treat your life as a special mission, because you can never be too prepared.

FACTOR IN YOUR ANSWERS

1. *If your life is a "Special Operation", what is the mission? How have you prepared to execute it?*

2. *When you find yourself held back with a negative mindset, what can you do to shift to a positive one?*

3. *Look at an activity or event coming up in the future. What contingencies should you plan for and what solutions would you provide for each one?*

4. *Think about a recent experience. Using the After Action Review approach, what went right and where are the opportunities to improve?*

+ CHAPTER 9

THE TRAINING FACTOR

$$m\ (T) = f\ (P^2 + \mathbf{t} + s + a)$$

Preparation has played a strong role in my life. From preparing to compete on the football field to training as part of an elite military team, I have always taken training seriously. And you should, too.

Training is a combination of learning and practice. You learn a skill or task and then practice until you've mastered it. Remember the equations:

Education + Practice = Experience

Education x Practice = Mastery

Mastery requires commitment. Commitment comes from passion, from embracing something with such energy that you won't let go. When you feel you have no more to give, you reach down and find enough to keep going.

Have you experienced that feeling in your life?

If you haven't, you have no idea what you're missing. I hope I can inspire you to seek that level of passion and commitment that sparks the most effective training program.

TRAINING = RELIABILITY + PREDICTABILITY

One of the reasons we train is to create consistent outcomes and meet expectations. The repetitive activity builds your work ethic, which builds your reliability. You've proven to do what it takes, and others know they can count on you. Training also creates predictable results. There's no guessing about the steps because you and your teammates have trained to the point of them becoming automatic.

Sales coach Larry Levine wrote an interesting article that compared selling to the game of golf. They are both individual sports, he wrote. "If you want to excel in golf, not only do you need to play the game, but you must consistently practice. The rewards don't come with every shot, every hole, or even every round."[1]

A golfer carries 14 clubs in his bag. Each one is a tool, serving a specific purpose. The pro golfer trains on each club, mastering the functionality for reliable, predictable results.

"In golf, the approach to every situation is different," Levine explains. "The courses are different, the conditions are different, there are obstacles requiring different strategies and different club or iron usage. Unpredictable conditions present things that are totally out of their control. Golfers can catch a bad break, get a bad bounce or a bad lie as they have to deal with it and recover from it."

If a golfer applied the concepts of Special Ops training, they would learn all those contingencies that Levine described. They would train to prepare to respond quickly to each one.

A solid training program allows for possibilities—for expecting the unexpected—like I explained in the previous chapter. You train to be prepared for various conditions and situations.

---

1 Levine, Larry, "Attention Sales World...Think And Act Like a Professional Golfer", LinkedIn, January 24, 2021. https://www.linkedin.com/pulse/attention-sales-worldthink-act-like-professional-larry-levine/

> **If you needed to tear down the aircraft in four hours and you did it in four hours and one minute, you failed.**
>
> —Kirk Keepers,
> Special Operato

You look ahead to deal with the foreseeable "What if's". And when you come up against a situation that you hadn't prepared for, you do an After Action Review, determine what you should have done, and add that to your training program. You are never done training. You can complete a program but there is always more to learn and room for improvement.

Remember Kirk Keepers, the member of Special Operations Forces I referenced earlier? Kirk appreciates the value of intense training. He and his fellow soldiers always knew what they were training for—missions where you had to count on one another without any doubt that every person would come through. They trained for predictability and precision, so that they were confident that every member of the team was prepared when it came time for a mission.

"We could load up eight aircraft and be in Africa in 72 hours, with almost no words spoken. We trained the same every time. We knew exactly what the standard was. If you needed to tear down the aircraft in four hours and you did it in four hours and one minute, you failed. You don't deviate from the standard."

The training addressed every possible contingency. "We'd go out to an aircraft on the water, sitting on a raft, and blow the doors. We look at things like the emergency exit. What hand around are you going to grab the rail with? You know things will happen, so you think of everything that is or could happen," says Kirk. He added that he taught his daughter how to change a tire. She asked why she needed to practice this skill. He told her, "You practice so you don't have to learn it in a stressful situation."

"Whatever and whoever you aim to be, you can't get there without training."

I told you earlier that Roger Clemens and I have discussed discipline and training on numerous occasions. We share a commitment to sticking to a regimen, no matter what it takes. Roger followed a disciplined training regime throughout his Major League Baseball career. He told me not long ago that his perspective on training was based on total dedication: "My only day off is the day I pitch."

He studied the batters he would face and conducted his own version of an After Action Review to see where he needed to improve.

"When you win, you win. When you lose, you learn. There's no such thing as failing," he said. "Remember, you will come out on the other side a better person.

> *"When you win, you win.*
>
> *When you lose, you learn."*
>
> —Roger Clemens, Former MLB All-Star pitcher

So maybe you're not a pro golfer, a Special Operator, or All-Star pitcher, but whatever and whoever you aim to be, you can't get there without a commitment to training.

THE POWER OF "WHY"

Motivation does amazing things. When you have the proper motivation, you can exceed expectations. You put in the time and energy, you reach farther and deeper into yourself. But you have to want something badly. You need that hunger to succeed in whatever venture you're taking on. Without strong motivation, training might not last longer than the session itself, as brief as a New Year's resolution. Without powerful motivation, you revert to your old, comfortable ways because your reason for improvement just couldn't bear the weight of the effort.

> *"Without powerful motivation, you revert to your old comfortable ways, because your reason for improvement couldn't bear the weight of the effort."*

You'd think that a life-and-death situation would be enough to motivate a person to make a change. A study of 52 lung cancer patients who had survived five years or more after treatment[2] showed nearly half of them returned to smoking as soon as within a year of their operation. I can't imagine how someone could free themselves of this life-threatening habit, only to slip back into it.

Similar studies have been conducted of patients who survived a heart attack or stroke. One out of four men failed to make lifestyle changes after recovering from a cardiac event.[3] Women, by the way, are more likely to adjust their habits to adopt healthier behaviors. But that's not really a surprise. Change isn't easy, but women seem inherently more flexible.

If you survived an experience that threatened to take your life, what would you do as a result? Would you make lasting changes? Only YOU know the real answer.

KNOW YOUR GOAL

You need a clearly defined goal when you embark on a training plan. Maybe you want to get stronger or healthier. You want to perform better at your job or in school. Whatever it is, make sure your "Why" is strong enough to drive you to achieve that goal. If you haven't yet determined your "Why", find it. You need motivation that's powerful enough to keep you on track to reach your goals.

There's a problem with some goals though. They're too vague. What does it mean to you to be in better shape? Is it shedding some pounds and losing a few sizes? Are you looking for more muscle tone?

You can start training with that objective in mind, but a goal needs to have four elements to be effective:

1. Defined (clear and written down);

2. Achievable (realistic);

3. Measurable (for accountability); and

2 Davison, A. G., & Duffy, M. (1982). Smoking habits of long-term survivors of surgery for lung cancer. Thorax, 37(5), 331 333. https://doi.org/10.1136/thx.37.5.331

3 Kulash, Tara, "25 percent do not change bad health habits after heart attack, stroke", St. Louis Post-Dispatch, August 15, 2013, https://www.stltoday.com/lifestyles/health-med-fit/25-percent-do-not-change-bad-health-habits-after-heart-attack-stroke/article_f30164af-2368-5cf5-8bdc-3f641a7607b8.html

4. Offering a reward for achievement (incentive).

A vague goal is like groping around in the dark—it's too easy to get lost. An effective goal is set with clear parameters for what you want to achieve and when. How many pounds do you want to lose? How much weight do you want to lift? What size do you want to fit into? You can lose 10 pounds and call it quits if you haven't defined your goal clearly enough. Maybe your training is intended to do better at your job. What does "do better" mean to you? Do you need to show up on time instead of strolling in a few minutes late each day? Are you aiming to complete more tasks in a day? If so, are you looking at the number of tasks you can finish or the quality of your work? Pinpoint your targets by going back to your "Why" and your goals.

REWARD YOURSELF

During my business journey, I moved on to Centex Destination Properties, a national homebuilder, where I took on the role of Vice President of Sales. I attended the annual sales rally for the first time. One of the awards recognized the Top Salesperson, who was presented with a Rolex. When I saw that watch, I knew I wanted one. More than that, I wanted to build my own sales organization to reward someone else with a Rolex.

I cut out a photo of the Rolex I wanted and put it on the wall in the sales trailer at the Centex community where I was selling homes. Every day, I saw that photo and it renewed my desire to do and be more.

> *"What do you want enough to motivate you to achieve your goal?"*

Four years later, I bought that $17,000 watch—two actually, one for me and the other for my top seller.

What is it you want enough to motivate you to meet that goal? The reward needs to be personal and meaningful so that it matters enough for you to work for it. Share your goals with other people to hold yourself accountable.

I once met with a sales team that told me their goal was to sell more in the coming year. I said, "Great! So if you make just one more sale this year than you did last year, you've met your goal, right?"

They looked at me with expressions that ranged from confused to absolute disdain.

"Yeah, I didn't think that was your goal," I continued. "So, let's be more specific."

From there, we discussed the sales volume and gross revenue. Once we had those numbers established, we configured a critical path for achieving the goal, based on meeting daily, weekly, and monthly markers. Daily action plans help you measure your progress and lead to achieving your weekly and monthly goals. If you opt for anything less frequent, you can get in trouble.

Set specific goals before beginning your training. Be clear on what you're training for. That's your target so make it one you can see. Create a detailed and concise agenda that outlines what you need to accomplish for your training. Keep that vision in your head to maintain motivation.

Establish a timeline. A goal without a timeline is a wish. When you announce a goal but don't attach a deadline or schedule, you fail to include the all-important accountability. Before long, you push off the tasks you should have completed and the opportunity to achieve your goal fades away.

Build a critical path. Map out a plan of actionable tasks that are necessary to hit your target. Your critical path should be your roadmap to success, so include anything and everything you can foresee. For each item on that list, ask yourself that all-important question, "What contingency should I account for?"

> *"When you announce a goal but don't attach a schedule to achieve it, you fail to include accountability."*

"Training isn't expensive. Ignorance is expensive. "

—Myers Barnes

TRAINING AND TRAINABILITY

Motivation is the major predictor of success when it comes to training. The stronger the impetus driving your change, the greater your success.

But there's another factor we need to look at: Trainability.

Think back to your classroom days. There was probably someone—or several someones—in your class who felt that the material presented wasn't important enough or relevant to them.

"Why do I need to learn American history? That's all in the past."

"When am I ever going to use algebra? I don't plan to be a teacher."

"Face it. I can't run a mile, so why bother?"

These types of complaints come from people who don't want to grow. They've already accepted the "Can't", which is more accurately a reflection of "Won't". When they put up that barrier, they release themselves from proving that "I can" is achievable. This mindset is a clear sign of being untrainable.

> ### *"A person who doesn't want to grow accepts the 'Can't', which is more accurately a 'Won't'."*

Trainability is something you hire for in a learning culture, so be aware. I don't care if you're considering a proven superstar. If that person isn't open to training, you don't want them. The "Know-It-All" is a dead-end in your organization. When evaluating candidates, use a battery of tests like we did in Special Ops to assess trainability.

I get that not everyone can achieve anything they want. But closing your mind to the possibility makes failure a foregone conclusion. Don't let yourself go in that direction.

TRAINING TO THE NTH DEGREE

The training for Navy SEALs and the Army's Special Ops is

among the toughest tests of strength, endurance, and perseverance anywhere. The programs are designed to eliminate anyone who isn't 100 percent prepared to deal with the tasks assigned to these forces. There's no room for even the tiniest hint of a weakness.

In his book, *"Make Your Bed"*, US Navy Admiral William H. McRaven presented the ten life lessons he carried with him from SEAL training. He explains how anyone can apply the lessons and gain from them. If you haven't read this book, please do it. It's short, but powerful.

The book's title, *"Make Your Bed"*, refers to one simple task that starts your day. It's what he calls "an incremental goal", a small step that leads to bigger ones.

McRaven also tells the story of his former SEAL instructor, Lt. Philip L. "Moki" Martin, one of the most physically fit individuals McRaven had ever known. A triathlete, Moki embarked one morning on his daily 30-mile bike ride, pedaling at his usual intensity of 25 miles per hour. So focused on his ride, Moki didn't see an oncoming rider. They collided. The other cyclist had minimal injuries, but Moki was permanently paralyzed from the waist down.

In the 35 years since Moki had been committed to a wheelchair, McRaven noted, "I never once heard him complain about his misfortune in life. Never once did he display an ounce of pity for himself."[4]

> **"Moki Martin's unrelenting pursuit of excellence didn't waiver, even when he could no longer walk."**

Moki Martin became a father and an accomplished painter after his accident. He also founded and still oversees the annual Super-Frog Triathlon in Coronado, California.

Moki would never give less than his maximum effort, no matter what he did. His unrelenting pursuit of excellence didn't waiver,

---

4 McRaven, Admiral William H., (2017), "Make Your Bed", (pp. 41-42), Grand Central Publishing (New York)

even when he could no longer walk.

THE COST OF *NOT* TRAINING

Myers Barnes is a sales coach who works with home builders around the country, including our Legacy team. As my own coach and mentor, Myers has worked with me since the beginning of my career in real estate. Like Coach John Fields of the University of Texas, Myers knows that mindset is critical to training—and that includes the person overseeing the trainees.

A learning culture can train you all day long but if you don't have a learning mindset on the receiving side, that training won't matter. The most successful individuals and teams are committed to ongoing learning. They realize there is always room for improvement.

On occasion, Myers gets pushback from a client who isn't quite convinced of the value of training. "What if I train them and they leave?" is the common question. He responds, "What if you don't train them and they stay?"

Myers has often told me, "Training isn't expensive. Ignorance is expensive." He's right. While you can't accurately measure the cost of not training yourself or your team members, you absolutely can measure the results when they are trained.

I challenge you to identify one tool you want to sharpen. Set yourself up with a training program to make it happen. Read Stephen Covey's "*7 Habits of Highly Effective People*" and Jim Collins's "*Good to Great*". Be clear about your motivation and hold yourself accountable for the follow-through. It might become a powerful habit that contributes to the sum of your Life Equation.

What are your training goals? How are you going to reach them? What factors are you thinking about right now for your Life Equation? The world is your classroom. You just have to show up and pay attention.

LIFE EQUATION LESSON

You will never complete your training. There is always more to learn. Embrace the opportunities. Welcome the chance to expand your knowledge, skills, and experiences.

FACTOR IN YOUR ANSWERS

1. *What training has provided you with the most lasting results? How and why did it succeed for you?*

2. *Who has been your most valued mentor? What has this person added to your life?*

3. *Have you mentored others? What does the experience give you? What have you learned about yourself from mentoring others?*

4. *What motivates you to train harder for something? Are you clear about your goal when you start?*

5. *To be effective, a goal must be: (1) clear and written down, (2) achievable, (3) measurable and accountable, and (4) offer a reward for achieving goals. Have you followed this process in the past? What is a recent example?*

+ CHAPTER 10

STARTING OVER AFTER THE MILITARY

From the time I was sixteen years old, I had a clear picture of my future. I saw the path I would follow to get into and then through West Point. I pictured serving my country in the military after graduation. I could see myself in everything from the camo to the dress whites, from marching in unison to serving side by side with my fellow soldiers.

What didn't appear in that view was my life beyond the military. I guess I figured that all that preparation for becoming a soldier and an officer represented everything necessary for my future.

And then I held our newborn daughter in my arms. Jordan was perfect. In her tiny face, I saw a future like I had never imagined. The enormity of being a father hit like an invisible tidal wave washing over me. I would be "Dad" to my little girl.

I looked from Jordan to my beautiful wife. Chris had been my rock, my compass, and my partner in life since the moment we shared that first dinner. And she had just given me the gift of a daughter.

That was 1999, and I so desperately wanted to be a good dad, one who would always be there for Jordan, to be her rock, like Chris has been mine. I wanted to give her a special life, and I wanted to make her proud of me.

That is when I began to wonder if the life of Special Ops was right for my family. I had overcome so much to become a Special Operator and be part of an amazing professional Army team, but none of the past mattered right then and there. My family is my strongest pillar, my greatest blessing and having them by my side is, by far, my proudest achievement.

MILITARY IN THE REARVIEW MIRROR

In 2000, when we learned a second child was coming, I made the decision to leave the military. I informed my battalion commander, Lt. Col. Michael Rose—a very difficult conversation—in June 2001. I know I've referred to "badasses" in this book, but this man was the toughest, most intense badass I have ever known.

I was leaving behind all that I had known for thirteen years, including military school and service, almost half my life thus far. I'd stepped up to face many challenges and channeled my competitiveness for the best possible result. I had earned the privilege of being part of an incomparable Special Ops team, serving with all kinds of people from all over the country. We shared a purpose and common goal of protecting America and one another, so that others could be free to enjoy whatever endeavors they chose in life.

> *"Some might feel that military life is restrictive, but there is comfort in knowing that you're prepared to respond to any emergency at any time."*

The bottom line is, I did not know what was ahead with a civilian career. You follow a precisely defined path in the service.

Every action, no matter how minute, is ingrained in you. While some might feel that this lifestyle is restrictive, there is comfort in knowing that you're prepared to respond to any emergency at any time, that all of your training has led to being the best soldier you can be. Right there, giving up that predictable routine, that's the toughest and most opportunistic part of leaving the military (the many people who helped shape my leadership experience not-withstanding).

SAVANNAH ON MY MIND

The next step in moving on was answering the question, "Where do we go next?" Chris and I talked about staying in Savannah, Georgia. We loved it but there was only one spot at Hunter Army Airfield in Savannah for a helicopter pilot and that had been as-signed to Bartt Owens. Meanwhile, I was going to be deployed to South Korea, one of the largest Chinook duty stations in the world. We had sold our home in preparation for the move, but Bartt's home was still on the market. I asked if he would be willing to switch assignments and after making one phone call, it was done. We went to Savannah and Bartt soon headed to Korea.

Later, we learned that Bartt had been killed in a training exer-cise off the coast of Korea. I don't remember that Chris and I ex-changed many words about our friend's death. But in our eyes, we shared one thought: But for the grace of God, that could have been me. Bartt left behind a great family and served his country well.

> *"With my service and my team*
> *still visible in the rearview mirror—*
> *along with the images of the Towers*
> *falling etched in my mind—*
> *I wondered if I should turn back."*

Just months after I left the service and while I was on military terminal leave, 9/11 happened. I had served since 1994, training all those years to respond swiftly and to lead my team on any bat-tlefield. My service didn't occur in wartime, but I remained ready and at my peak mentally and physically. And with my service and my team still visible in the rearview mirror—along with the images of the Towers falling etched in my mind—I wondered whether I should turn back.

At the same time, my second daughter was just two weeks old when our country was struck by terrorists. I had looked at Jensen as I did when Jordan was a newborn, with the same desire to give her everything I possibly could. And that meant doing my best as a civilian who had garnered such a valuable store of experiences, knowledge, skills, and resources. I had also earned an MBA from Embry Riddle Aeronautical University by attending night school while stationed at Fort Campbell, Kentucky. In fact, I sent in my final thesis while doing desert ops training at the Fort Irwin National Training Center in California, in the early days of the Internet. Remember dial-up?

AN AWKWARD TRANSITION

There's a balancing act that many veterans experience after leaving the military. While you're on active duty, you have processes to follow, outcomes to deliver. Everything is outlined, every action is planned to precisely follow a process.

Then you're faced with civilian life, one that doesn't define expectations in an orderly manner. As a member of the armed services, I had stability. I knew what to expect from each day and each action, what steps to take, having been trained to respond instantly and accurately.

At the end of your service, you transition with what is called "terminal leave". You accrue vacation days over the years you're serving. You serve so much that you never use the time. There's no "use it or lose it" option, and I had accrued quite a bit.

The government offers veterans the services of headhunters who work with you to find the next place to land beyond the boundaries of military service. While the headhunters were seeking out opportunities, I took a little detour from the job search—or so I thought.

" **Knowing nothing about something had never stopped me before.** "

NOT SOARING SO HIGH

I recalled a fellow helicopter pilot who had also left the service and was living in Savannah. Major Jeff Jepson flew Blackhawks while I flew Chinooks. He had helped Chris and me find a place to live when we first came to Savannah, two and a half years earlier. I recalled that Jeff was in charge of a real estate community that had a very desirable golf course.

I called Jeff out of the blue. "Hey, I've got some family coming in. Could you possibly get us on your golf course?"

"Sure!" Jeff answered. "And stop by after you finish."

After a very satisfying round on the links at Southbridge, I found my way to Jeff's office. We chatted a bit. He asked what I was up to and I told him I was looking to get started on my civilian career, whatever that would be. He introduced me to Mark Hall, the son of Glen Hall, who founded the company Jeff was working for, Hall Communities. The family-owned business developed communities in the South's most desirable vacation destinations. Jeff and I swapped some flying stories, and then we all chatted a bit about my search for a career change.

A few days later, Jeff called me with an invitation to join Hall Communities. They were getting ready to launch a new destination property in Savannah and both he and Mark thought I'd be an asset to the team. He also added, "If you like Savannah, real estate is a great career."

This new community would span more than 3,000 acres, so it was no small project. I discussed the opportunity with Chris. She thought I was crazy. All these headhunters were offering logistics jobs with guaranteed income and I was seriously considering a sales job that would be paid solely on commission. Still, knowing nothing about something had never stopped me before. I took the risk and decided to give it a try, even though I knew nothing about sales or real estate. But I believed in my ability to do this—and to do it well.

> *"Knowing nothing about something had never stopped me before."*

After passing the real estate license exam, I began selling homes at Southbridge. Truth be told, I began TRYING to sell homes. It was slow going.

I learned everything there was to know about the homes and the community. I shared my knowledge with interested buyers but wasn't closing deals. I had spent my entire adult life to this point achieving the goals I set for myself. I flew troops to execute covert missions. I had survived the very real simulation of being held captive. And I fought my way back from the injuries suffered in a car accident to pursue my goal. But here I was, unable to close a deal on a house.

Then came Myers Barnes. Myers is a coach, trainer, wizard, guru, and master of selling new homes. The Hall family had a long-standing relationship with Myers, who came in and provided ongoing sales training. Jeff handed me a copy of one of Myers's books, "*Reach the Top*".

In typical fashion, I didn't just read the book. I devoured it. I highlighted key points and flagged pages with sticky notes. I experienced one "aha" moment after another and felt certain that Myers had unlocked the barrier to my sales success.

Although Myers's book had completely changed my perspective, I hadn't yet met the man. When he eventually came to do sales training for our team, I was that eager learner at the front of the room. Apologies to the rest of the people who were there.

Myers in person is even more remarkable than Myers in writing. It only takes one time to see Myers coach to see and feel his belief that the sales process works and matters.

When I finally met Myers in the flesh, he asked, "Did you read the book?"

I showed him my copy with all the notes and sticky notes. He looked at it, flipped through the pages, and smiled at me. "I've never seen anything like this!" And that began a coaching relationship that continues to this day. It also led to a major opportunity, but we'll get to that in a bit.

HERE'S THE THING ABOUT SELLING

Sales knowledge is important to anyone. At some point in time, you sell yourself—to a college or university admissions officer, a love interest, an employer, a client, to name a few. Whether selling a product, service, or yourself, having sales skills is valuable.

Myers Barnes taught me invaluable lessons about the sales profession. Selling is a process. To this point, I was fully accustomed to training in processes, so this realization was a welcomed relief. I reminded myself in those early days of home sales that I had committed to this career change, just like I had committed to going to West Point. With that same dedication, I would put all my energy and focus into the challenge.

Selling is a mission—and I can totally embrace that concept. But I was going about it all wrong. I spewed a litany of features about the homes I was selling. But I had failed to achieve a critical first step in the mission. I hadn't gained the buyer's trust. I was looking at selling as a transaction, not a process. If they don't trust you, they won't buy from you.

Myers coached me to ask questions, some of them hard questions. It's "the art of discovery", uncovering needs, wants, and triggers. I needed to spend time getting to know a prospective buyer before rushing into showing them beautiful homes to buy.

A proven process is a beautiful thing. Do this, this, this, and this, and here's what will happen.

A REAL RECIPE FOR SUCCESS

Ed, a mechanical engineer who was driven by precision, was teaching his daughter-in-law, Lori, to make baklava, a sweet pastry with layers of phyllo dough and honey. It's a tedious process, and one he took great pride in mastering. Ed went through each step in

"Whether selling a product, service, or yourself, having sales skills is valuable."

his recipe with her. Lori suggested that they could skip one step and Ed replied, "You follow the steps as they're written. If Step 7 says 'Stop and go to the bathroom', you stop and go to the bathroom."

Sales is like that. Not the bathroom part, the step-by-step part.

Look at it as a path that a buyer is following, from "I wish" to "I want!". Remember me talking about David Camp, the master of art and science in strategy? He explains that a buyer's path is like navigating a boat through a canal with a series of locks. You can't proceed until you've successfully put one section of the water behind you. "Don't open the next gate until you can close the one behind you," says David.

A sale is the result of a collision between magic and logic—or, as David calls it, "art and science". The magic/art side is discovery, he says, asking the questions to find out a person's drivers. These are the emotional factors. Conversely, the logic/science is the linear process, taken one step at a time, to get through one lock before proceeding to the next one.

> **"A proven process is a beautiful thing. Do this, this, this, and this, and here's what will happen."**

In my first few months of attempting to sell homes at South-bridge, I had focused on the logic side: how much I knew about the community and the homes. Facts, facts, and more facts. I hadn't yet explored the magic, the relationship building part of the selling process. With Myers's help, I learned to identify techniques and procedures to understand why this buyer was talking to me or even showed up to the community in the first place. He coached me on uncovering what the buyer was looking for and then how best to "demonstrate" a home. Instead of first whetting their appetite for the impressive home they were about to experience, I had been rushing them to show off the model home rather. It's a kind of sales foreplay—what we call "the impact tour" to try the community on for size and experience what it would be like to live in that neighborhood. Fall in love with the area before falling in love with the home.

With this training, I became more proficient at the process of selling a community and homes. I courted my prospects with questions that demonstrated my interest in helping them find not just a home, but the right one. That meant listening and even being willing to say at times, "Maybe this is not for you." And I kept asking until I felt ready to show them homes, moving through the canal, one lock at a time and in the right order—even backing them up through the locks as needed.

"I _wanted_ buyers to challenge me. It was a buying signal."

To my joy and amazement, the process worked! I was selling homes. Every sale uncovered more questions to ask, and I sharpened my responses. With the success, I wanted more training. Myers taught me that objections are predictable, so I studied and prepared myself for the inevitable pushback. In fact, I _wanted_ buyers to challenge me. It was a buying signal that they were seeking more information.

Meanwhile, the Hall family was planning to launch the other resort community with a Greg Norman Golf Course and a Southern Living Idea House Program. Glen Hall, the family patriarch, approached Myers for his advice on where to look for a sales manager for the project. Myers told him, "Philip is your man."

"Do you think he's ready?" Glen asked.

Myers had my marked-up copy of his book in his briefcase. He pulled it out and showed it to Glen, with all the paper tabs sticking out. "This is your leader, Glen. You don't need to go looking. He's right here."

THE WADE INFLUENCE

Not long after I was promoted, the Hall family sold a percentage of Savannah Quarters to a division of Greg Norman's firm, known as Medalist Golf Developments. With this joint venture came the relationship with Playground Destination Properties, a division of Intrawest, that had just started serving developers outside of their own family of Intrawest resorts. This gave their pipeline of prospects and owners more resort communities options to sell. Medalist had an existing relationship with Intrawest Playground, known as Playground Destination Properties, and that's where I met another inspiring individual.

Wade Shealy was Playground's Southeast Vice President of Sales and Marketing with eleven resort communities under his watch. Wade, a Georgia boy, is perhaps the best salesperson I've ever known. It's not because he's slick. He understands buying behavior and he reads people expertly. Wade is a genuine guy, who started his sales career with a summer job selling books for Southwestern Book Company, door to door in remote areas where you would think failure is a foregone conclusion.

During his training in Nashville in 1976, along with thousands of other eager college kids, Wade had difficulty memorizing the sales pitch. What he did have was a powerful desire to prove himself and to show the naysayers that he could do more than just sell. He looked at the people on the stage and asked what it took to have that spot. "That's the top salesperson from last summer," Wade was told. Right then, he decided he would one day occupy that spot.

On his first trip, Wade was partnered with another college student, Blake, who had been the #1 salesperson the previous year. The duo was sent to New Hampshire, where they rented a single room from a woman who had been contacted by the company. Wade had no car, just his supply of books and some pocket change. He needed to make sales to get money so he could eat.

The first morning, Blake dropped off Wade in a residential area, at least by New Hampshire standards, which means the houses could be spread far apart.

At the first house, a woman answered the door. Wade tried to remember the speech but forgot to ask her the key question. He was selling kids' books and failed to find out if she even had any kids. Florence was an older woman, but she ended up buying three sets of books for her grandchildren. While they were talking, Florence's 80-year-old mother came in and asked what he had. She liked the large-print dictionary and bought a complete set.

He was motivated and kept going from house to house until 8:45 that night. Wade sat at the curb where Blake had promised to pick him up at 9:00. He waited and waited, but Blake didn't come. Wade gave up and walked back to the house where they were staying, lugging along his sample case. He flung open the bedroom door, ready to confront Blake for leaving him out there. The room was empty but there was a note on his bed.

"Can't do this for another summer but you'll do great. Blake"

Without any transportation, Wade kept going. He went for weeks alone, hitchhiking from one town to the next. At the end of the summer, he earned that spot at the top of the sales chart. Without a car and out in the boonies, Wade achieved his goal.

Wade is high on my list of the best badasses I've known. He is relentless but with a charm that makes his unstoppability a pleasure to watch.

"If you have a deep desire, you can overcome a lot of things," Wade told me. "My destiny wasn't based on Blake. It was on me."

> ### *"If you have a deep desire, you can overcome a lot of things."*
>
> —Wade Shealy
> Founder and CEO, THIRDHOME

Wade went on to become an extremely successful resort developer. Along the way, he frequently reconnected with buyers who had bought vacation homes from him. Many of them came back to Wade a few years later to sell the home because they didn't use it enough. That trend sparked an idea. He reached out to a few

"If you have a deep desire, you can overcome a lot of things."

—Wade Shealy
Founder and CEO, THIRDHOME

to see if they would like to be charter members in a club where people shared their vacation home with other members. He started THIRDHOME in 2010. Just like his success with selling books door to door, Wade made the best of an opportunity. Today, THIRD-HOME has 13,500 properties in 99 countries.

To this date, Wade and I are still working together.

THE NEXT BIG MOVE

Under Wade's tutelage, I rose to Director of Sales and Marketing in the Southeast Region of Playground Destination Properties. I was managing business development opportunities and participating in the launch of a condominium phase in a major resort community in Sandestin, Florida. This was the first phase in Baytown Wharf village on the bay side of Sandestin. I believe it was one of the best sales teams in the world. The properties themselves were an exciting product—great resort location and gorgeous condos in a village setting. Chris and I bought a home and settled in with the girls, enjoying the tropical life.

In December 2003, I got a call one night from a former colleague who had left Playground to join Centex Destination Properties, another massive developer. Arnie told me that Centex Homes was adding a resort division to its portfolio of residential real estate. As Vice President of Sales and Marketing for Centex Destination Properties, he was growing his sales and marketing teams to cover the Central Division, one of four divisions: East, Central, West, and Hawaii. Arnie and the Division President invited me to come to Texas to work on resort properties that Centex was acquiring in Houston, Austin, and Dallas.

Chris, the girls, and I loved our life in Florida, so leaving there wasn't an easy decision. Austin, however, was one place that my New Yorker wife had visited with me while I was at West Point. We went to the beautiful hill country and Lake Travis. We loved it there and I knew she would consider it.

I told Arnie that the only way I was returning to Texas was if I could come home to Austin. He agreed. I took the job and moved my family to Texas. I was excited to go back home, and I also knew he was a smart, motivated, and honest guy.

Within the first year of relocating, I successfully built a sales team for a Centex lakefront community that was taking shape. The selling system was working and the folks at the Dallas headquarters took notice. One day, Joe Arcisz, Division President, called to ask me to fly up to Dallas and meet with him. I didn't know exactly why, but when a superior officer gives you an order, you follow it, no questions asked.

As we sat in the conference room, Joe explained he was impressed by me, by my work ethic and my sales success. He wanted my leadership for his entire division. He planned to announce that I was replacing my former colleague as the sales leader. He felt I was better suited at the time to evolve and grow with his other functional area leadership. He called Arnie to deliver the news and made the announcement within days.

> *"Don't look back at your life with regret.*
> *Instead, look ahead at your opportunities."*

Although excited for this next step, I felt terrible that I might have cost Arnie his job. Then I remembered what Wade taught me. My destiny—and Arnie's—is not based on anyone else. It is based on my choices, performance, and results. Mine and mine alone.

GUIDE YOUR OWN JOURNEY

We are the result and sum of our choices, good and bad. Don't look back at your life with regret. That's a useless emotion that gets you nowhere. Instead, look ahead at the opportunities, and use your Life Equation to keep you focused on achieving your goals.

Where is your journey going? Remember that you are your sole navigator. Your Life Equation is your map.

LIFE EQUATION LESSON

When you hit an obstacle, don't stand there and stare at it. Find a way to get where you're heading. And only look back to affirm how far you've come.

FACTOR IN YOUR ANSWERS

1. *Would you prefer to stay with what is familiar or step outside your comfort zone? What's the reason for your preference?*

2. *Have you had to restart or redirect your life at any point? What was the biggest challenge for you?*

3. *How do you approach a challenge? Do you consciously follow an approach?*

+ CHAPTER 11

THE PASSIONATE PEOPLE FACTOR

$$m \; (T) = f \left(\mathbf{P}^2 + t + s + a \right)$$

You hear a lot about finding your passion. And it's very true that people who discover and follow what really matters to them are happier and more successful. After all, isn't true success a measure of your happiness—and NOT vice versa?

When I first started to calculate my Life Equation, I knew that passion and perseverance would be part of it. I've never done anything half-assed. What's the point? You only short yourself in the long run.

> *"True success is the measure of your happiness— not vice versa."*

Have you known people who go to work to collect a paycheck? With the one life you have, do you want to spend it dragging yourself along without ever knowing the joy of real fulfillment? That shouldn't be an option. It's too big a price to pay. Think about the areas in your life where you are making compromises because you haven't uncovered your passion. You can spend time, getting no return on it, or invest your valuable time in something that sparks you. I choose to pursue what I'm passionate about—the tasks that intersect with my passion and belief of changing people's lives. We all have 24 hours in a day. How you use that time is your choice.

THE TIME COMMODITY

Think about time like this. You're standing in a long line of people. Someone goes down the line, handing each person 24 hours.

"This is yours to spend as you see fit," says the Time Giver.

Some race off wildly, not sure where they're heading but feeling rich with the gift. At the end of the 24 hours, they look back and wonder how it passed so quickly. And what meaningful thing did they have to show for it?

Others look at the stack of 24 hours and ponder how to best use them. They use one hour pondering the possibilities. Then, they go off and do the things that will give them the most satisfaction. When the 24 hours have passed for these people, they feel content in what they achieved.

Time is a commodity to be invested. You can reap the rewards of smart choices or fritter away the time with nothing to show for it.

Time is the one precious commodity you can't grow. No matter what you do, time passes. Remember that when you find yourself killing time. Here's another equation for you:

Time + Passion + Effort = Great Things!

WANT TO BUY A BIBLE?

This powerful energy is a force within you. Every individual has their own unique motivators to finding their passion.

In the previous chapter, I told you a little about my one-time boss and hugely successful entrepreneur, Wade Shealy. I want to share the details of the training he experienced in his first sales job because it paints a more vibrant picture of what he accomplished and overcame.

Wade was a poor kid from South Georgia. He was studying Landscape Architecture at the University of Georgia and he needed to find a way to pay for his education. As you may recall, he got a job selling bibles, books, and dictionaries door to door. The company hired college kids from all over the country and had them come to Nashville for training.

Wade didn't have a car but caught a ride from Georgia to Tennessee. He walked into the Nashville War Memorial Auditorium where he was one of 7,300 kids there for training. Wade looked up at the presenters on the stage. Dressed in great suits that Wade admired, they brimmed with confidence. Their passion ignited the crowd of kids eager to be just like them.

"The kids were standing in their seats, cheering for those guys," Wade remembers. "I remember thinking, 'I want to be one of those guys one day.'"

He asked someone what a person had to do to be one of those presenters on the stage.

"You've got to be a top salesman and then come back and recruit friends and build a big sales organization," he was told.

Undaunted by the challenge, Wade said, "I just decided, this is what I've got to do, figured out how to do it, and made it work."

The trainers didn't share his optimism. Wade couldn't memorize the sales speech, which the trainers considered an essential accomplishment for these raw salespeople to achieve success. But their doubt in him fueled Wade's drive. "They didn't know what was inside of me. That's the unknown factor."

As I explained in the previous chapter, in Wade's first summer doing sales—without a car and very little money—he managed to make his way from one small New Hampshire town to another. At the end, Wade became the top salesperson. He didn't recite the

> **Sometimes people see others they want to emulate.**
>
> **The image of that person gives them a visual for the goal.**
>
> —Wade Shealy

sales pitch he was taught, but instead spoke genuinely to each customer. Not only did they buy books from him, but many did even more. They drove him to the homes of their friends, neighbors, and family, giving each of these potential customers their seal of approval on this young man.

Wade returned to college that fall and changed his major to Business. The following summer, he brought 25 friends with him to the sales training that was taking place in Oklahoma that year. The summer after that, he brought 75, and in the fourth summer, he had more than 200 kids in his selling network.

After graduating from college, Wade became a trainer for the company. He wore one of those nice suits he had admired years before and drove a sports car like the role models that first sparked his excitement.

"Sometimes, people see others they want to emulate. The image of that person gives them a visual for the goal," Wade told me.

Later, Wade rose to Vice President of Sales for Playground Destination Properties, the selling subsidiary of a national resort property developer, which is where I met him and where we did great work together. From there, as I mentioned previously, he went on to develop his own tremendously successful business, THIRDHOME.

THE BIG NUDGE OF THE LITTLE VOICE

Maybe you haven't had the eye-opening vision of what you want. It's not always one "aha" moment. It can percolate inside you, fed by the positive experiences over time. But the little voice inside your head attempts to keep you on track, if you have the discipline and open-mindedness to just accept that there's something of value.

"Have the courage to follow your heart and intuition. They somehow already know what you truly want to become. Everything else is secondary," said Steve Jobs.

HOW DO YOU RECOGNIZE YOUR PASSION?

To answer that question, start by answering two others:

1. *"Do you show up with fire?"* You should feel so excited about what you're doing that it feeds your energy rather than draining it.

2. *"Does your 'Why' keep you going?"* Your motivation needs to be so compelling that you only need to remind yourself of your purpose to get a jolt of excitement.

Passion sparks curiosity, so passionate people are always reading and learning. Every week, my team dials in from all over the Americas and we start out with "Monday Learnings". We take turns leading the meeting. Whoever is leading that day chooses the subject. The leader of the week starts with a daily read, a dose of motivation to get people thinking, which is part of our learning culture. They articulate a related topic of conversation and support it with audiovisual and other materials to drive home and experience the meaning of the daily read. Maybe it's about attitude or overcoming objections. The leader reinforces the message by applying it to a practical experience. Finally, we all talk about experiences over the previous week and what we learned from it. Someone might present something they've read that feels valuable to the group. Whatever it is, I know that my week is going to start out energized because I'm in the company of truly impassioned people.

FIRE UP YOUR FUTURE

In 2008, the economic downturn took its toll on a young, single mother, Julie Krumholz. She had been working for a residential developer in the Austin area, handling the details and tasks of property contracts. When the housing bubble burst and sales slowed down, she lost her job. Not long after that, Julie came to see me. My company, Legacy International Resort Properties, had just been hired to drive the sales and marketing for a residential community near Austin, and Julie thought she'd be an asset to our efforts.

I told Julie that we weren't ready to hire for that project yet. I struggled with that thought, because there was something about Julie that made her stand out in my mind. I brought her back for more interviews and every time, I tried to figure out how to fit her into the organization.

But then it was clear that I didn't need to fit her in. I just needed to welcome her. So I did. Julie came on board as Customer Operations Manager in 2009, helping us to define and enhance the customer experience.

Julie was passionate about real estate and the way it changed lives. She glowed with energy when speaking with homebuyers. It had nothing to do with a sales pitch. She loved what she was doing. Customers knew Julie was genuine, like Wade Shealy had been with his book buying prospects. Julie's customers trusted her honesty and her desire to help them. Changing lives was her passion and her Why.

"Any person can do a nine-to-five job, but if they don't have passion, they won't end up with true success. Passionate people are engaging, likable, and affect everyone around them in a positive way," said Julie, who raised three kids on her own. Her middle child had an auditory processing disability. Julie advocated for her but also set her up for success by teaching her daughter how to be her own advocate. "It's more than being a cheerleader. When you're sincerely passionate, you have the right mix of pulling people in, actively listening to them, and having a 'can do' attitude."

The people on my Legacy International Team know about my Life Equation. I guess I talk about it a lot.

Initially, the Life Equation was:

$$m\ (T) = f\ (P + t + s + a)$$

Translated: The motivated team is the function of the right

people with the right training plus a shared strategy and accountability for everyone.

Julie suggested to me one day that the Life Equation needed something more.

"It's not just the people," she told me. "It should be Passionate People. You should change that factor to P^2."

Bingo!

Julie was right. It's not just about building a team of people. Without passion, neither the individual nor the team will ever perform to their true potential. By elevating the factor from P to P^2, my revised Life Equation showed that "Passion" exponentially enhanced "People".

PS: I've had many people with input on these factors over the years and this was the only one we changed. This one's for you, Julie, a real badass.

PPS: If you're tired of my "badass" references, you haven't experienced the awe-inspiring impact of one. In my view, this distinction is a badge of honor.

> **"It's not enough to bring together a group of people as a team.**
>
> **Without passion, neither the individuals nor the team will ever perform to their true potential."**

IT'S THE PERSON, NOT THE JOB

Many amazing people have come into my life. I've mentioned a few already, including Red McCombs. His wisdom has been a long-time reminder to me of what is possible when you don't give up—on yourself as well as on others.

The Texas billionaire came from humble beginnings. He grew up on a farm in the 1930s. The hard life there taught him he needed to do more to fulfill his ambition. He turned 18 in 1945 and enlisted in the Army. Red literally fought his way to becoming

> "When you're sincerely passionate, you have the right mix of pulling people in, actively listening to them, and having a 'can do' attitude.

—Julie Krumholz

the Army's heavyweight boxing champion of Korea, although he'll tell you it was just luck.After his military discharge, Red enrolled in the University of Texas and went on to law school there.

"I knew I was not by any definition a top student, so where did that leave me?" Red wrote in his biography, *"Big Red: Memoirs of a Texas Entrepreneur and Philanthropist"*. "I finally realized that a career in law was going to be too confusing for a guy like me. It's hard to explain how significant a change that was. I'd always just assumed that law school was going to be my ticket to get there—wherever 'there' was. But I really hadn't understood what the practice of law was about. When I did figure out just exactly what an attorney does, it was like I fell into a black hole for a day or two. I was really angry with myself."

Red pulled himself out of the gloom. He found his way to a Ford dealership and discovered his passion. He learned that the average car salesperson sells about ten vehicles a month. Red set his sights higher: sell one car a *day*. For three years, he sold 31 cars a month! He went on to build his own dealership, which spawned more. He established Red McCombs Automotive Group, which employed at one time more than 1,000 people who all follow the company motto: "Driven to Serve".

> *"The average car salesperson sells about ten vehicles a month.*
>
> *Red set his sights higher. For three years, he sold 31 cars a month."*

As I mentioned Red co-founded Clear Channel Communications in 1972, which he sold in 2008. That company is now known as iHeartMedia, a multi-billion-dollar corporation.

Why am I telling you all this about Red McCombs?

The man is legendary. His passion is limitless. His ability to take on and meet challenges is unmatched. At 94, he is still going into his San Antonio office. His enterprise is largely run by his daughter, Marsha Shields, but Red's presence remains inspiring to his team and me.

Marsha learned a lot from her dad. Like him, she never shied away from hard work or obstacles. In spite of being a McCombs, she built sweat equity, working her way through just about every role in every business, starting with the car dealership. Marsha was given opportunities, but not entitlement. Her dad was a role model for hard work, and she learned her lessons well.

Marsha's biggest lesson over the years was recognizing that Red hired a person for whom they were, not to fit a job. I learned that same lesson and used it on many occasions since I first launched Legacy International. If I hadn't been enlightened enough to understand this valuable notion, I would have missed out on having some exceptional people working with me.

"His goal was always to find the smartest person, the hardest working, most aggressive people he could. When he would find a person like that, someone who was going to make a difference, he would hire them, even if he didn't have a specific job. He wouldn't let someone just go by," said Marsha during one of our last interviews with her father.

Red would meet capable people right out of school or maybe after five to eight years of working in a specific job. They wanted to come in and talk to Red for career advice. Marsha says her dad would often see their potential before they did. It was like a superpower that enabled Red to see success in someone's future. Or it was his insightful character that sensed their passion and knew the value of it.

> *"His goal was to find the smartest person, the hardest working, most aggressive people.*
>
> *When he would find a person who was going to make a difference, he would hire them, even if he didn't have a specific job."*
>
> —Marsha Shields, on her dad, Red McCombs

PASSION FOR HIRE

In the 1970s, Red was looking for someone to take on a management position in the company. Gary Woods came to see him. Gary could see right away that he had to sell himself. He told Red he would work the first year without pay, to show what he could do.

"Gary was very academic, very measured in his approach," Marsha remembers. "Dad was all risk, all fun, all pushing the envelope. The two of them had balance and made a great organizational team."

Gary eventually became president of McCombs Enterprises.

What struck me most was when we did one of our last interviews in person. It's not just these stories but his quote.

"If you can see someone who has talent, ability, and motivation, you hire them," Red often said. "It's the person, it's not the job."

HONORING RED

Red McCombs has been one of the most impactful forces in my life, outside of my own family. He gave me his brand of Texas wisdom, delivered with a look that told me, "This will make sense someday." And it always did.

The man never let an obstacle stop him but managed not to step on anyone along the way. His life story is a master class in living life the smart way. When I last sat with Red McCombs in his office, he was 94 years old and confined to a wheelchair. But this inspiring man still stood taller than anyone in the room, spoke with the power, charm, and brilliance of a man whose wealth is most accurately measured in experience, not dollars.

I didn't know at the time that this would be the last one-on-one meeting with Red. His daughter, Marsha, knew that her father needed to pull back from the office, a place where he had come for almost 20 years. Prior to that, Red went to his office at the

"**Remember that killing time is a crime— and you're both the victim and the perpetrator.**"

auto dealership, Monday through Saturday. On Saturday, he would clean off his desk to prepare for the coming week. And he spent Sunday with his family.

In that last meeting, just before Red stopped taking meetings, he told me about the importance of time. He said, "We all get 24 hours a day. That's it. No more, no less. It's up to you how you use that time. At the end of the day, when I go to bed, I think about what I did that day. What did I do that was worthwhile? Was I a good person? Who did I help? Every day, counts, Philip. Make yours count more."

I am thankful for Red and his family, for the opportunities they have graciously shared with me. Most importantly, I cherish this man for seeing something in me that was worthy of his time.

SPARK YOUR PASSION

No matter where you are in your life, I hope you're living it passionately, that you wake up every morning fired up to take on the day and make the most of it. Remind yourself that killing time is a crime. No amount of punishment or remorse will bring back that lost time.

While you're at it, surround yourself with people who share your spirit. It takes the right people to win. If you are weighed down by people who aren't driven to achieve, you allow this burden. They will hold you back, presenting their own reasons why you should slow down or, worse yet, "be more realistic". Place yourself in the company of passionate people and the "can do" attitude will compel and propel you.

Building teams is at the heart of what I've woken up for each and every day of my adult life. Have you yet discovered the passion that ignites your action? Don't postpone the search for your "Why". It's too important to let it fall off your priority list.

LIFE EQUATION LESSON

Dig in and find that underlying power that drives you—your "Why". Hold onto that passion. Remind yourself every single day why you get out of bed and do what you do. Stoke that fire. It will be your energy source as long as you do.

FACTOR IN YOUR ANSWERS

1. *Who are the most passionate people you know personally? What is their passion and how does it motivate them?*

2. *What sparks your own passion? What is the "Why" that ignites your excitement? How do you show that you're passionate about something?*

3. *Have you had to "go through the motions" on something that was someone else's passion but not yours? Could you have made a different choice or taken a different approach to make it a more meaningful experience for you?*

+ CHAPTER 12

THE ACCOUNTABILITY FACTOR

$$m\ (T) = f\ (P^2 + t + s + \textbf{a}\ )$$

Who is to blame for what you haven't yet achieved? Your parents, your teachers, your friends, your boss? All of the above?

By this point in the book, you know the answer is you, right? You chose your friends and your job. You have the power to leave them behind when they're holding you back. You didn't choose your family but you are certainly in charge of how you allow those relationships to impact you.

Let me remind you, your life is the result of your choices. Among those decisions is the choice to accept responsibility. Why does it matter?

1. When you hold yourself accountable, you're more effective and productive. You don't waste time looking for others to blame. You get right to problem-solving and implementing solutions.

2. You are a strong leadership model for others. Your actions impact those who follow you. Do you want a group of finger-pointers playing the Blame Game on your team?

Integrity is doing the right thing when no one is looking. Holding yourself accountable—doing what you've said you will do—eliminates disappointment, prevents the need for excuses, and allows for predictable results.

On Day One at West Point, we were taught that only three responses are acceptable to an upperclassman's order: "Yes, Sir", "No, Sir" and "No excuse, Sir." It's really that simple.

THE TIE THAT BINDS

Accountability starts with you. Total accountability happens when you hold others to the same solid standard for responsibility as you do for yourself, and they do the same with you. When you decide whom to put in certain roles, be sure they understand that accountability is a team effort. Then, cultivate a culture that supports this universally accepted approach.

Your teams—whoever they are and whatever binds you together—function best when each person lives up to expectations. To appreciate this, look at the opposite scenario. Do you have a friend who habitually bails out at the last minute or a family member who can always be counted on to NOT be counted on to do as he or she says? When you think about that person, also think about this: How does this lack of accountability on their part directly impact you? Disappointment comes when expectations aren't met. Then it grows into resentment—and that's the relationship crusher.

> *"If you don't have the right people in the right places, there is no one to hold accountable."*

Turn this view around and take a good look at yourself. Are YOU the one who isn't taking ownership of your "misses": missteps, mistakes, and miscalculations (underestimating your time or resources, for example)? Be honest.

> *"Disappointment comes when*
> *expectations aren't met.*
>
> *It grows into resentment—and*
> *that's the relationship crusher."*

PROUD DAD MOMENT

My oldest daughter, Jordan, has always been passionate about learning—and maintaining independence. She never let anything slow her down, including a dad who, I admit, tried to steer her in various ways. She refused help, so insistent to succeed on her own. With that independence came accountability.

"Part of being independent," she admitted, "was realizing my choices would impact me. I need to be ready for any consequences, in charge of my own mistakes. Throughout college, if I missed an assignment, that's on me and I would work hard to make up for it."

From a very young age, Jordan knew she wanted a career in engineering. She made decisions to stay on that track, which meant studying hard to the exclusion of a teen's social life. She is about to graduate from Colorado University with the mechanical engineering degree that has been her goal for so long. Jordan has a job waiting for her at the general construction firm where she interned for two summers. She will be doing exactly the job she has wanted. And, by the way, while earning honors status in college, my laser-focused daughter also wrote and published a novel. Cross that one off her list, another thing she managed to achieve before her dad.

I always loved Jordan's intense commitment to her goals and the strict accountability that kept her on course. I admire her tenacity. Truth be told, I also respect her independent nature that she so stubbornly grasps. So, when a young person complains in my presence about how their parents didn't support their dreams or they weren't given opportunities, I'm not sympathetic. Success does not come to the weak.

Some people find excuses. Some people find a way.

—Wade Shealy

EXCELLENCE INSTEAD OF EXCUSES

Back in Chapter 11, I told you about Wade Shealy. Now a highly successful entrepreneur, he started out selling books door to door as a college student in a remote New Hampshire area. When his sales partner abandoned him—taking with him the only transportation Wade had—he could have easily called the headquarters to relay his dilemma. He could have used the valid excuse that he had no transportation and quit. Instead, he found a way to get rides from kind customers, who would drop him off at a friend's or relative's house. Along with the ride, they gave Wade a referral, which helped him hit the top of the sales chart that summer.

"Some people find excuses," Wade said. "Some people find a way."

Where do you want to put your energy and focus?

"HERE'S WHY I FAILED"

Excuses are a waste of time. An excuse is a long-winded way of saying, "Here's why I failed" and hoping to be absolved of your error. It doesn't matter if you believe you have a good reason for your failure. It's still chalked up in the loss column on the scoreboard. But when you convert that outcome into a valuable lesson, you've actually made progress.

Conversely, a solution says, "I learned."

> *"An excuse is a long-winded way of saying, 'Here's why I failed.'*
>
> *A solution says, 'I learned.'"*

I have accountability tenets I adhere to in both my work and personal lives:

1. I will not ask you to do anything that I wouldn't do myself.

2. Don't come to me with a problem unless you can also present a possible solution.

Now ask yourself, who would you rather have on your team: someone like Wade Shealy who doesn't make excuses, or a person who is looking to point blame anywhere but where it truly belongs?

ACCOUNTABILITY AND THE ART OF LEADERSHIP

Accountability starts at the top. Leaders must hold themselves responsible for what's happening in their organization. Not long ago, my office manager overlooked a task I had asked her to handle. As she apologized, I thought about why she missed this one thing.

"It's my fault," I told her apologetically. "I didn't offer the right training. Let's work together to fix that."

What happens on my watch, whether I'm directly responsible or not, is on me. A strong leader accepts responsibility for mistakes. I've stood up in front of my team on numerous occasions, admitted my mistake, and accepted the consequences. But then we, as a group, immediately look at how to move on. How do we fix the error? How do we avoid repeating it? As I said before, I will never ask someone to do something that I wouldn't do myself—and that includes admitting to a mistake.

Whether you are leading one person or many, be a solid role model for accountability.

> *"I will never ask someone to do something that I wouldn't do myself— and that includes admitting to a mistake."*

AFTER ACTION REVIEW

In the military, an After Action Review (AAR) followed every exercise or mission. The purpose was to learn and improve from every action. We'd bring the stakeholders together and look at what happened, good and bad. Explore the steps that delivered a positive contribution and seek to understand the factors that didn't help. The AAR gives insight that you can apply to future actions. The AAR also contributes to the decision process, providing additional insight when determining multiple courses of action. The military teaches that you should always have a back-up plan and be keenly aware of contingencies. Your goal is to allow for predictable results—something that is valuable in any area of your life.

My Legacy International Team regularly conducts an AAR after an event or activity. No excuses and no blaming are allowed in these sessions. We examine how an outcome compares with our expectations. Sometimes it's great, other times, not so much. It's not a time to pat ourselves on the back, but to recognize there's always more work to be done. We have open, honest discussions and it's interesting to get various perspectives. In the end, we walk away feeling positive and ready to apply our knowledge to the next opportunity, handling it even more proficiently.

WHY PEOPLE MAKE EXCUSES

Let's back up a bit and understand why a person is compelled to make an excuse. A child makes an excuse to avoid getting in trouble. For example, a friend's son told her, "I accidentally failed my math test."

"Oh, well," she responded with her stern "Mom" face, "at least you didn't do it on purpose."

Did the excuse get him out of trouble? Not one bit. In fact, his attempt at softening the blow of the failure made it worse because he also failed at taking ownership for not preparing well enough for the test.

The AAR for this student and his mom could go like this. How did he "accidentally" fail? If he didn't study enough, then you document how he prepared for the test and how he can improve that process. The AAR is summarized with an action plan, which sets the lesson in motion.

In the end, the student learns that facing up to a mistake is an opportunity to learn from it, rather than getting reprimanded (although he probably got some of that, too).

Your team members use excuses in a similar manner—to avoid

the repercussions for failure. That punishment could be just a gently delivered admonishment or as severe as being terminated. Remember that your workers also want to have your respect and admiration. They might feel that owning up to a mistake makes them unworthy.

Switch the scenario and focus on the reward for taking ownership. Eliminate that guessing. Discourage excuses and encourage solutions.

FIXING A HOLE

My youngest daughter, Jensen, was playing in a junior golf tournament when she was a sophomore in high school (bragging rights here—she's an exceptional player, nicknamed "The Hammer"). Jensen was playing great, leading the pack. I was caddying for her and enjoying every minute.

On the second day, in the second round, and on the back nine, she shanked it off the tee box. I was stunned! But The Hammer, unruffled, gave me that look I will never forget. She said to me, "Dad, we will never play that hole again."

There I was, not yet realizing I was learning an important life lesson from a 16-year-old.

What she meant is that this particular scenario would not recur. The weather might be different, the grass could be maintained differently, and her mindset might change as well. Her point was, "Get over it and move on to the next hole. Let's not live in the past."

She did just that, without losing composure. Her game returned to her stellar level. She would ultimately finish second in the tournament, not because of that particular hole but due to another player absolutely crushing it on the second day.

Later, Jensen and I did an AAR about that shot. Jensen knows she can always get better and she welcomes lessons. She told me I was obsessing over that one shot. "If you keep revisiting a bad shot, then you get frustrated," Jensen told me. "All those things get into my head and block my focus. Ok, that happened and I can't change

" **When mistakes happen—and they always do—learn from them.** "

it. How I carry myself from here is going to change the outcome of my score on the remaining holes and my mindset on everything. I need to stay focused on the objective, which is winning the golf tournament."

To this day, Jensen continues to make me proud, competing as an athlete-scholar, competing at the highest collegiate level. Who knows what the future will bring for this talented, young woman.

When mistakes happen—and they always do—learn from them. Look back and analyze the action. Apply that experience to what comes next to move closer to predictability.

COMMON EXCUSES AND HOW TO MANAGE THEM

Although excuses serve one purpose—avoiding blame—they are delivered in a variety of ways. When you can recognize the underlying meaning, you're prepared to deliver a response that fosters accountability, with the dual achievement of gaining essential predictability.

"It's not my fault."

This is the classic finger-pointer response. Don't jump into this game. There is no winner because the mistake has happened. You can respond by saying, *"No one is blaming you. We simply need to figure out how to solve it and make sure it doesn't happen again. Do you have any suggestions?"*

Addressing it this way puts the responsibility back on the one denying blame. Once they realize you are not playing the Blame Game, you shift attention to solving the problem, not justifying it.

"It's not my job."

Ok, I'm going to tell you that this one really ticks me off. When you are part of a team, you pitch in as needed. Every leader, manager, and team member should model the right example by going above and beyond. I've stuffed envelopes, cleaned up after events, and shoveled dirt when extra help was needed for real estate events. Early on in my flight career, I pumped jet fuel for my team's helicopters when it was my turn to handle logistics. Remind your people that you never ask them to do something that you wouldn't do yourself.

To the one who claims, "It's not my job", reply, *"It's not among your assigned duties for your job title, but it IS part of your job as a member of this team. When each of us can be flexible and helpful, we all win."*

If you haven't seen the movie *"Miracle on Ice"*, the movie that depicts the story of the 1980 U.S. Olympic hockey team, put it high on your watch list. The team fought the odds to beat the heavily favored Russian team for the chance to play for the gold medal, which the Americans won. Their coach, Herb Brooks, was a masterful leader. Brooks insisted that the jerseys not carry the name of the player who wore it. His intention was to reinforce the belief that each person was playing for a team, not himself. In this case, it was the USA.

I support that approach. The team, as a unit, is at the forefront, not an individual. We have job titles on business cards and org charts. In the workplace, you lose that title. Collectively, our job is mission critical and it is not your name on the jersey.

"No one told me...."

Ignorance of the law is no excuse. Maybe no one gave the deadline or clearly communicated expectations. Rather than shrugging off the responsibility, the individual should go in search of the missing pieces. You want thinkers and self-starters in your group, people who take initiative rather than waiting to be spoon-fed.

Respond to the "No one told me" person with, *"I'm sure it must have been frustrating. How could we have made the expectations clearer for you?"*

Once again, you redirect the problem-solving to the unknowing worker. You make it clear you are not looking to blame anyone for what happened but are instead establishing a process for moving forward.

"I didn't have enough _____."

Often, this blank is filled in with "time". It's understandable to accept "good enough" when the clock is ticking. However, from a proactive standpoint, it's far better to give a heads-up well in advance that something is moving off-course rather than under-delivering. No one likes bad news, but they really hate it when it comes after the fact. By communicating changes up front, you succeed at managing expectations, whether it's good or bad news. Skip right to the response, *"How could we make sure you have enough _____ in the future?"*

"I thought _____ was doing it."

Playing dumb is never a smart move. Assumptions, if not clearly defined and all included in decision making, are a sign of a communication gap. A You should have a system of checks and balances, a built-in factor that assigns clear responsibility to avoid guesses that lead to mistakes, delays, and oversights. Your comeback in this instance is, *"We need to confirm, not assume, and/or reconfirm and update. There's always the possibility that something changes and we need to adjust. Let's look at the process to make sure that step is always included."*

> ### *"Assumptions are a sign of a communication gap."*

Your goal should be to get rid of assumptions because they lead to problems. That's the only way you can achieve predictability that leads to smooth maneuvers and successful outcomes.

If any of your team members don't accept accountability after repeated attempts to encourage it, sit down and have a frank conversation. Be clear that the resistance to being responsible is not an option.

THE "NO EXCUSES" ENVIRONMENT

Teaching accountability is a common challenge for today's leaders and managers. The "No Excuses" environment should be a goal of every organization, business, group, and family.

> **You can spend time placing blame or you can be effective. It's one or the other.**

A strong leader builds accountability in the team. Start by clearly communicating expectations. Then assign key performance measures that allow them to see their progress in the After Action Review. Teach them to take ownership of their challenges as well as their successes. Instill in them that "No excuses, just solutions" is the rule. Enforcing this rule instills accountability while also encouraging them to strengthen their problem-solving skills. I've found that it also eliminates a LOT of traffic in my office!

You can apply this approach at home as well as work. Be clear about expectations and hold your kids to the standard that you want them to embrace. You don't need a formal After Action Review. Just have a family meeting. The objective is the same.

Remember that you can spend time placing blame when something doesn't go as planned or you can be effective. It's one or the other. Blame is like a hot potato, tossed from one team member to the next. Ultimately, it lands on one person, who may or may not be deserving of it. All this finger-pointing does nothing to fix the mistake. It just delays the fix.

THE ACCOUNTABILITY TWO-STEP

There are two simple ways to minimize errors and strengthen accountability:

1. **Set clear expectations.** Make sure that everyone involved understands the common goal. A critical path details every step and should be integral in all of your plans. It also provides the measuring stick to evaluate performance.

2. **Deliver helpful feedback.** Good or bad, offer feedback on the process of getting things done in your group. In the AAR, discuss suggestions for improving the process and/or results, and document the action.

Accountability is the thread that weaves your team together. Each person should be accountable to their teammates as well as themselves. The West Point Cadet Honor Code states, "A cadet will not lie, cheat, or steal, or tolerate those who do." Cadets are duty-bound to follow "The Three Rules to Live By", asking themselves three questions:

1. Does this action attempt to deceive anyone or allow anyone to be deceived?

2. Does this action gain or allow the gain of privilege or advantage to which I or someone else would not otherwise be entitled?

3. Would I be dissatisfied by the outcome if I were on the receiving end of this action?

Answering "yes" to even one of these questions means the action violates the Honor Code.

GET THE TRAIN ON THE TRACK

Accountability is the **center of gravity**, the core of everything else. You can have great people, train them, and have the "Why", and with all that, you build a powerful train. However, without accountability, you never get the train out of the station. It chugs along slowly or derails. Ultimately, whatever set of factors you have put into your Life Equation, "Accountability" is the one ingredient that MUST be included.

In that single item, you reflect on where you've been, where you are today, and where you're going. Without those reference points, you leave too much room for error, once again, allowing for a lack of predictability.

> *"Own your failures. Learn from them.*
>
> *Each mistake is an opportunity to learn and become a better person."*

If everyone could include the "a" of Accountability in their LIfe

Equation, the world would be a better place. Picture a society where those responsible took responsibility for their actions and choices, if less time were spent placing blame and more on creating solutions. The more you encourage accountability in your own sphere of influence, the closer we get to that better place.

Own your failures. Learn from them. And demonstrate to others that each mistake is an opportunity to learn and become a better person. And never forget those three simple phrases: "Yes, Sir; No, Sir; No excuse, Sir."

LIFE EQUATION LESSON

We all make mistakes. They are only failures when we fail to learn from them. It's equally important to acknowledge your responsibility. Seeking someone to blame will not only delay the solution but also deludes you into believing your own excuses—and that's a dead end because you can't grow from that position.

FACTOR IN YOUR ANSWERS

1. *Do you hold yourself accountable? What are examples of when and how you did this?*

2. *Who is someone in your life who needs accountability? Why do you think they resist being answerable? How could you help to instill the quality in this person?*

3. *What was the last time you failed to deliver on an expectation? Did you offer an excuse? If so, what was it? Looking back after reading about "The Accountability Factor", how could you have handled the situation by holding yourself responsible?*

+ CHAPTER 13

SUM OF THE PARTS

You've come this far. Have you thought about building your Life Equation? Have you discovered why you need to do it?

You have one life, but it represents countless opportunities. You can take each one as it comes, but I guarantee you, without a plan, you'll miss some big ones. You underestimate the value of some and simply overlook others. And who knows what those missed chances might have brought you.

> *"Life presents countless opportunities.*
>
> *You can take each one as it comes, but without a plan, you'll miss some big ones."*

Maybe you weren't motivated enough to get off the couch. If you had, you might have met someone or learned a lesson that would have otherwise become life-changing.

You didn't push yourself to do better in school or at work. Imagine if you had done just a little bit more. What would your life look like today?

You didn't think a goal was within your reach, so you abandoned it. Maybe if you had believed more in your own potential, you'd have transformed a dream into reality.

Rarely do you get a chance for a do-over. Once the possibility has gone by, it may never come back. You have actually "killed" time. There's a finite amount of time in your life, and no one knows exactly how much remains. Can you afford to waste any of it?

The past won't change. The future can. But only if you design it that way.

> *"The past won't change.*
>
> *The future can.*
>
> *But only if you design it that way."*

START CALCULATING

I don't expect you to live by my Life Equation, but you can use it as a starting point.

$$m\,(T) = f\,(P^2 + t + s + a)$$

A motivated team is the function of passionate people (P²),

who are consistently trained (t),

armed with a detailed and resourced strategy (s)

that holds one another accountable (a).

If you've read this book from the beginning, you know why I chose these factors. If any or all of them feel right to you, you've got a head start on your Life Equation.

Let's quickly revisit those factors so you can see how they come together and decide if any should be included when you formulate your own Life Equation.

MOTIVATED TEAM - m (T)

My Life Equation was built from a desire to change people's lives by leading others to help in this journey. From serving my country to developing a business that supported the goals of my team members and brought people to their dream of home ownership, that's been a lifelong passion. To achieve it, I knew I needed to lead a motivated team who shared my vision.

Then I asked myself, "How do I build a motivated team?" The answer came to me over time. At West Point, I learned what it means to be a strong leader. In the military, and especially during my time in Special Operations, I refined the skills by leading teams on missions with a defined purpose. And then in my post-military career, I continued to learn what it takes to be a successful leader.

You can't "have" a motivated team. You build it. You can step into a leadership role in a club, business, or even a group of friends. Taking it on doesn't make you a leader. Your actions do.

If teams are going to be important in your future, I recommend that you look at building MOTIVATED teams.

PASSIONATE PEOPLE - P^2

After years of working side by side with passionate people, it's a fact that this type of commitment and energy fuels success like nothing I've ever seen. Not even money. Especially not money. That's a commodity you trade. Passion is an infinite power that launches a person from self-doubt to confidence and purpose. A strong leader can ignite passion, but they need to be impassioned with a "Why", first and foremost, or there's nothing to spark.

"Passion is an infinite power that launches a person from self-doubt to confidence and purpose."

I'm a passionate person so I need to surround myself with other people who are energized. I find that their positive attitude is a real plus in the moments when you experience self-doubt or need a jolt to restart your thinking.

" **Taking on a leadership role doesn't make you a leader.**

Your actions do. "

TRAINING - t

Training isn't just training for a sport or a job. It's the ongoing pursuit of growth. Let's all agree that nobody's perfect. So, we all have room for improvement—building knowledge, skills, habits, and character.

Where do you want to focus your growth? Whether it's personal or professional development, training is a valuable component in a Life Equation. Approach your world like a Special Operator: Always learning and training with the dedication to precision and commitment to pushing through in order to be predictable and gain solid results. Make it your mission to become and stay sharp, because that will truly make you unstoppable! Never dismiss or underestimate the importance of this innate desire to always be learning and growing. You can be proficient, even far beyond your peers, but there will always be room to be better. Hold tightly to the desire to keep learning.

STRATEGY - s

I put Strategy into my formula because years of military training have ingrained in me that you don't dive into anything without a plan. Remember the seven steps of MDMP, the After Action Review, and the critical path? They all lead to developing a strategic approach that takes "possibility" into consideration and ensures that you weigh consequences into your choices.

Failure to plan and execute this key step leads to wasted time and compromised results. You wouldn't decide to have a major event—like a wedding, reunion, or fundraising gala—without planning every step. You figure out what you want to happen and then work backwards to determine the steps, timeline, and respective resources to get there. You also factor in contingencies, like "What if it rains?"

Strategy is essential for your Life Equation because building one forces you to examine your ideas and work through the details, step by step by step. And as you look at each step, you see how one leads to another or possibly presents a problem you need to consider.

Take the time to plan for contingencies ahead of time so you're not frantically trying to get out of a situation. Proactive is always better than reactive! Taking time to plan for contingencies proactively enables you to be more predictable, reliable, and trustworthy.

ACCOUNTABILITY - a

This is the differentiating factor in making progress. Without full accountability, nothing else matters. You allow gaps where integrity can slip away. You have leaks that are masked with excuses, temporarily disguising the hole but not fixing it.

Thomas Paine, the 18th century activist and author of *"Common Sense"*, wrote, "A body of men holding themselves accountable to nobody ought not to be trusted by anybody."

> ### *"Without full accountability, nothing else matters."*

If you can't own up to your own wrong choices, you are destined to repeat them. Once you've rationalized a mistake, you set a precedent that it's okay. "It wasn't my fault" magnifies whatever you did wrong. It shows you lack integrity.

Holding yourself and others responsible for their actions is not a punishment, but an act of true leadership. When you find yourself looking for an excuse, stop. Use your brainpower to look for a solution. And it starts by acknowledging your mistake. "I did this but I'm going to do this to make it right."

Think about the importance of doing this. You don't leave the sour taste of an excuse hanging out there, for you or the person you're feeding it to. Instead, you accept that you are human and made a mistake, but also have the integrity to want to repair the damage.

> ### *"Do what you say you're going to do, whether or not anyone else is keeping score."*

C.S. Lewis described integrity as doing the right thing when no one is watching. You're not looking for accolades, but living up to your own high standards for honor and ethics. Do what you say you're going to do, whether or not anyone else is keeping score.

It's a gut check that requires you to stay true to yourself and the people around you. Without the ability to hold yourself and others accountable, you lack strong boundaries. It's like taking a leap while attached to a bungee cord. You experience a momentary thrill but you'll only go as far as the elastic allows you. Then you bounce back to where you started from. Don't be at the mercy of limits that come and go depending on the strength of your conviction. Establish firm boundaries and stick with them.

START YOUR OWN EQUATION

This is how and why I chose my own factors. Yours may be very different, depending on your personal goals, your "Why", values, or the stage where you are in life. You need to evaluate what's going right, what needs adjustments, and where you're stuck.

What or who is holding you back? You need to be clear on that. It's not pointing fingers, but creating awareness.

> *"It's no one else's fault that you haven't reached your potential.*
>
> *Stop blaming others."*

Even if you incrementally get better, we all have gaps. Building and following your own Life Equation will help you fill in the gaps. If you improve 1 percent a day—which should be easy if you're paying attention   at the end of the year, you'll have increased 365 percent. At a minimum, your focus on following your personal formula will help you be better. Remember, it's no one else's fault that you haven't reached your potential. It's not because of your parents, teachers, friends, bosses, or significant others. It's you! Stop blaming others.

You have the power to make choices. You can choose to follow the direction that others map out for you. They might even be the right ones. But if you haven't taken a deep dive into what you need, want, and expect in your life, you'll never know.

YOUR LIFE IS THE SUM OF THE PARTS

Your Life Equation will guide you to making the right decisions, if you stick with it and if it's a formula that has been carefully planned. The factor on one side of your Life Equation must equal the sum of the factors on the other. Anyone can say $2 + 2 = 5$, but it doesn't. Your personal Life Equation has to add up. If there is a factor missing, you won't get where you want to go.

When you have identified the right elements and you measure your choices against this scale, you'll save yourself from so many missteps that pull you farther away from the success you deserve.

> *"Your personal Life Equation has to add up. If there is a factor missing, you won't get where you want to go."*

LIFE EQUATION LESSON

Your life is the result of choices, behaviors, and actions. You are the only one in control of it all. When you invest in building and following a Life Equation, you become the leader of your future. Whether your leadership grows from there is your choice and your opportunity. Be the sum of the parts you choose!

FACTOR IN YOUR ANSWERS

1. *My Life Equation was designed to guide my leadership so I wanted to build motivated teams. What would be your own purpose?*

2. *What qualities and beliefs should factor into your Life Equation? Why are they important to you?*

3. *What life lessons have influenced you the most? Why have they been so impactful?*

4. *It can take awhile to perfect your Life Equation. If you were to formulate one right now, what would it be?*

+ CHAPTER 14

START BUILDING YOUR OWN LIFE EQUATION

Starting to frame your Life Equation doesn't require you to drop everything and commit an entire day to thinking and planning. Take one step at a time. Build it carefully and thoughtfully. "Starting" is momentary, like crossing the starting line and a baby taking its first step. It's a beginning, and it's progress.

Commit to building your solution. Once you've begun, schedule time to work on your Life Equation. Schedule and use 15 minutes a day—before work, at lunch, or in the evening. Work on identifying your factors and why they matter. It's different for everyone. If you're working through your youth, in college, starting or changing your career, defining your adulthood, rely on others to help you identify your active adulthood. Revisit your Life Equation frequently as your life grows and changes—either as a reminder of what has gotten you this far or because you need to make adjustments to move further.

Test it out. Mathematicians and scientists spend years exploring theories. They formulate an idea and test it. You should do the same. Apply the factors to your life immediately, even before you have perfected your Equation. If you've decided that removing self-doubt is essential, work on achieving that goal while you continue to build the other values. Remember, one step at a time is still progress.

Be indestructible, indispensable, and unstoppable. Don't let others hold you back. Shake off the naysayers. Keep your eye on the target. Use your Life Equation as a roadmap to keep you on course.

I've spent every page to this point explaining why you need a Life Equation and how mine has helped me. I've detailed the factors in my Life Equation.

Now, it's your turn to pull your own factors together.

Here's a process to get you started on building your Life Equation.

1. Make a list of the beliefs that have steered you to this point.

Whatever words you live by, write them down so you can see them.

"Work hard."

"Never bite off more than you can chew."

"Underpromise and overdeliver."

"Treat others the way you want to be treated."

In the 160th SOAR Regiment, we lived by the motto, "Night Stalkers don't quit." Words have power when you believe in them. And if you don't believe in them, find the right ones.

> *"Words have power when you believe in them.*
>
> *And if you don't believe in them, find the right ones."*

2. **Rate the value of each belief to the quality of your life.** Score yourself on how firmly you live by it.

3. When your list is complete, ask yourself **which life lessons need to be left behind** so you can move forward. Then, build a new list.

4. **Look at the underlying values expressed in the life lessons you've kept.** Those are factors that belong in your Life Equation.

COMMIT TO THE VALUE OF CHOICE

Choose to change where you live or work, what you're studying, and who shares your inner circle. Weigh each one against how they align with your goals. Let go of toxic relationships that either impede your progress or don't contribute to it. Don't let negativity weigh you down.

Choose to be the person you want to be by holding tight to your values. When you stray from there, you open the door and it stays ajar. That means you'll stray again because you've created an opening. Fight the urge to go against what you've deemed as your core values and goals. Your conscience is a powerful thing. Listen to it.

Choose to stay mindful of your life mission. Have you stayed focused on your goals? Is your progress what you expected? If not, examine your choices and actions, and ask yourself, "Why?" Never allow complacency to slip into your life. It's a virus that can attack your willpower and motivation. It can dissolve your resolve.

Once you build your Life Equation, hold it close. Use it daily.

If I can leave you with one thing, get a Life Equation and win. Leave the world a better place and make every day count. And if you want to be indestructible, indispensable, and unstoppable, start now.

BLESSED AND MINDFUL

I've been truly blessed in my life. Although I'm not one to question these gifts, I do take stock of what I have and how I got here. This journey was marked with challenges. I survived a crash at 16 only to discover that 30 or so minutes of unconsciousness would change my life trajectory.

But without that experience, I would not be where I am today. I have an amazing wife and two daughters who have taught me what it means to give and get true love. I had the honor of serving our country alongside soldiers who taught me the true meaning of teamwork. I've built a business with the help of others who mentored me, supported me, and occasionally gave me a much-needed reality check—sometimes accompanied by a much-needed kick in the ass. They empowered me to ultimately serve THEM on a mission to change lives.

Continue your journey to becoming Indestructible, Indispensable, and Unstoppable! Find more guidance, insights, and advice at www.philipjalufka.com.

Philip Jalufka

ACKNOWLEDGEMENTS

This book would never have been accomplished without the guidance and help of some very special people.

To my wife, Chris, for almost three decades, you have offered your unwavering support of my mission to change lives…from countless moves in the military to raising the girls to being my co-founder and partner in every business decision we make….#WinningWithChris

Jordan and Jensen, my amazing and very unique daughters, you both will do great things with your strong focus and competitiveness. I don't say it enough but you make me proud by just being who you are.

To my parents, I work harder every day to make both of you proud.

Dad, your voice isn't loud but your words are powerful. That was one very important phone call and I can't imagine what my life would have been if we hadn't spoken that day when I was about to give up on a dream.

Mom, I've been blessed to have the love and wisdom that you have given me throughout my life. You taught me kindness, respect, and the art of giving.

I am thankful for my Grandma, who instilled in me the importance of hard work and always having faith, hope, and love. Love endures all.

I must also thank Myers Barnes, my coach, mentor, and friend for so many years. It was his suggestion to write this book and his commitment to a sales process that helped me achieve success in my career after the military.

To Red McCombs and Marsha Shields, I cannot express the depth of my gratitude for believing in me.

Pearl and Coach John Fields, you taught me valuable lessons about partnership, training, competing, and understanding people—insight that will stay with me forever.

Roger Clemens, whether we're kicking butts on the golf course or kicking back, your friendship always gives me an added boost of badassery.

To the many amazing professionals who helped me realize the dream of Legacy International, you continue to inspire me to chase higher standards: Mandy Van Streepen, David Camp, Jake Jalufka, Cass and Carrie Brewer, Staci Winbush, Julie Krumholz, Steve Guy, Kay Hogge, Larry Claybough, Ashley Rust, Stephanie Kelly, Allan Schweinberg, Bob Collins, and so many others.

To my West Point classmate and real estate strategic partner, Harry Adams, we still have more great work to do together.

Greg Anderson (and Pat and Jim) for your friendship and for inspiring me to be part of something bigger in applying to West Point.

Wade Shealy, my friend, your indomitable spirit is a thing of beauty!

Jeff Jepson, thank you for the opportunity that changed my life. I am forever in your debt for restarting me in the right direction.

I am also humbled and thankful for the relationships I've been privileged to cultivate with business leaders and visionaries. Gary Keller, working with you and your team is an honor.

Haythem, I appreciate our time as business partners and the continued friendship.

To Larry, our years of seeking, pursuing, and maximizing opportunities have been greater lessons than any master's degree.

Jay Papasan, Jason Abrams, and April Murphy, your ideas were the final touches I needed to reach this point.

Finally, I extend my heartfelt appreciation to the service men and women and their families for keeping us free while we strive to keep America the greatest place on earth and influence the rest of the world; freedom is not free...I love and appreciate every one of you.

ABOUT THE AUTHOR

Philip Jalufka is a veteran of the U.S. Army's special operations, West Point graduate, author, and business leader. From a car accident that nearly ended his life to a series of difficult challenges, he has learned to stay true to a vision and become an inspiring leader.

ARMY VETERAN

Jalufka proudly served his country as a commissioned, special operations aviation officer in the US Army. Captain Jalufka flew the Chinook helicopter and led highly specialized military teams.

Prior to his military service, he received Bachelor degrees in Economics and Political Science from the United States Military Academy at West Point. While serving in the U.S. Army, Philip earned an MBA from Embry Riddle University.

ENTREPRENEUR

Philip currently serves as CEO of Legacy International, a company he founded and cultivated to worldwide success. Legacy International is a residential and resort sales and marketing firm that specializes in executing sales platforms and processes for home builders and developers. He has built a network of world-class strategic partnerships with a single underlying goal: Changing people's lives.

With Philip's real estate and sales leadership, the company represents an active portfolio of more than $1B in annual sales revenue.

In July 2018, Philip organized Legacy Performance Capital (LPC), an asset management firm that now resources four to five micro-market real estate ventures per year, with a current center of gravity in Texas and a portfolio valued at $500 million… and growing.

In September 2020, Philip announced that Legacy International executed a Builder Developer Services Expansion Initiative with the #1 real estate firm in the world, Keller Williams (KWRI), once again demonstrating real estate leadership.

PHILANTHROPIST

Philip lives by the ideal that, "At the forefront of all we do, the greatest gift we have is the ability to serve and/or give back!"

As a veteran of military service, Philip is a proud supporter of Heroes For Freedom Foundation, a non-profit organization dedicated to helping veterans and first responders. Since 2008, Philip and the Legacy Organizations he leads have been raising money in a variety of ways. A percentage of every dollar made from sales at all the engaged residential communities is contributed to the Foundation in order to resource various Warrior events and personal needs throughout the year. This initiative allows *every* Legacy Team Member to know they are changing lives in meaningful ways.

FAMILY MAN

For nearly 30 years, Philip has been joined, supported, and sometimes challenged in his life pursuits by his wife, Chris. Their marriage is a true partnership of love, respect, and shared values. They have two daughters, both currently in college, who have demonstrated their own unique strengths and paths to personal success.

"His is a language of competence, of being able to talk, interact, listen, and learn through all kinds of direct lenses in just about every situation.... A small-town Texas boy raised on the kind of core family values that the greatest generation was weaned on, with personal responsibility, service, and commitment taking the lead, Philip Jalufka cut his teeth on the football field, parlaying his mantra, 'no excuses, just solutions' into what he calls his Life Equation for success."

—Cindy Clarke, Venü Magazine

Continue your journey to becoming Indestructible, Indispensable, and Unstoppable! Find more guidance, insights, and advice at www.philipjalufka.com.

57776027R00136